A Shitload of Practical Uses for the Most Flexible Word in the English Language

Written by a Shitty Author; Illustrated by a Really Shitty Artist

This Page Intentionally Left Blank For Your Shit.

We literally have a lotta shit to cover, so let's get to some introductions and other legal shit first!

Only one intro?

Shit no!

There is so much shit to cover, and for so many different groups, I just had to have more than one intro, if for no other reason than to justify your spending $12.42 on this POS. Most readers will report this book on their expense reports or deduct it from their 1040 under education.

What a crock of shit.

But, hey, more power to you.

SALES SHIT

If you want to buy shitloads of **SHIT** for your school, gift season, or other event, visit www.theshitbook.com for Deep Shit discounts.

ACK-ACK

Thanks to Kathy Myrtle of the Type House for being the only person willing to have her real name associated with this pile of shit.

interpact press

ISBN: 978-0-9628700-7-1
Printed in Thailand *(Cause it's a shitload cheaper.)*

seminole, florida

Dedication

To the folks of Whistler, whose shit inspired this shit, and who know more practical meanings for the word than anybody else on planet Earth.

Shitty Taxonomy (aka T.O.C.)

How can you talk shit unless there is grammatically correct organization of how shit works? That's what a taxonomy is: An organized way of looking at shit.[1] Imagine if there were no taxonomy of shapes? There would be no difference between a circle and a dodecahedron. That would be bad. The periodic table is a taxonomy. If there were no taxonomy, we wouldn't know how we are related to the Great Ape and the starfish. We have to have organization to make sense of the world around us. So, right or wrong, this is what I came up with. Shit is so fluid and dynamic, I don't expect these guidelines to hold up over time, but I hope it's more than just a shitty first attempt. In the meantime, it will do.

---

1 Here "shit" is used to reference any possible subject. Again, the incredible flexibility of the word shit is exemplified here because shit can mean absolutely everything … or nothing at all.

Shit from Kindergarten to Dementia

Kids know shit when they hear it.

Daddy says shit, and Mommy tells Daddy to cut that shit out of his language in front of the kids. But he does it anyway, especially with the bases loaded in the bottom of the ninth and the Yankees blow it. Shit!

Babies know shit. I smeared diaper shit all over my walls at eighteen months … or so my mom tells me. Every baby discovers their shit tastes like shit.

Four-year-olds know shit.

> HONNNEEEY! DID YOU GIVE JUNIOR A CHOCOLATE BAR TO CALM HIM DOWN, OR IS THIS BROWN STUFF ALL OVER HIS LIPS AND FACE SOMETHING I DON'T EVEN WANT TO KNOW ABOUT!

A lot of them say shit. The first time they say shit in front of Aunt Libby, mommy grins weakly, pulls Amanda's arm out of her socket and tugs her into the kitchen for a lecture. The first time seven-year-old Christopher says shit in front of Sister Mary Catherine, he gets a mouthful of Ivory soap mashed into his molars and Christopher blows 99.44 percent pure bubbles for a solid week. Shit!

By the time boys are nine and girls are nine and a half, shit is a regular part of their vocabulary. They do it to impress their peers and shock their elders; but no matter. They have begun to learn the finer nuances of shit in the English language. No shit, Parents;

no matter what you do, shit is an active part of their speech – unless of course, you are a Seventh-Day Adventist, and your kids are terrified of hell and brimstone and fire and shit … then they're shit out of luck anyway.

Get used to it.[1]

Shit is perhaps the most multifacetted word in English, and it seems to me (and the seven million other people who helped write and edit SHIT) that we might as well, as CSN&Y suggests, teach our children well. Let's teach 'em how to use the word shit properly:

- When it's OK to say shit.
- When it's not OK to say shit. (Think Catholics and Ivory soap.)
- How to say shit with one, two and up to seven syllables.
- How shit can be any part of the English language; noun, verb, participle, gerund, animal, vegetable or mineral.
- How to create their own shitty words to expand the scope and depth of shit in English.
- How to properly teach younger siblings and septuagenarians the proper use of shit in most day-to-day situations.

So, Parents and Teachers: embrace SHIT. Either we teach the kids properly, or they will use shit willy-nilly, and then the English language will really be up shit's creek.

Let's all help American education and avoid another generation of dumb shits.

– *The Shitty Author*

---

1 *Psycholinguistic* studies have demonstrated that profanity and other taboo words produce physical effects in people who read or hear them, such as an elevated heart rate. This fact is seen by some as evidence that reclaiming of words such as *queer* is a valid way to remove its power. The offensiveness or perceived intensity or vulgarity of the various profanities can change over time, with certain words becoming more or less offensive as time goes on. For example, in modern times the word *piss* is usually considered mildly vulgar and somewhat impolite, whereas it appears in the King James Version of the Bible where modern translations would use the word *urine* (2 Kings 18:27; Isa. 36:12) or *urinate* (1 Sam. 25:22, 25:34; 1 Kings 14:10, 16:11, 21:21; 2 Kings 9:8).

Why Shit?

Because we all do it. We all try to pretend we don't. We can't say it on TV and we teach our kids it's dirty.

Remember when we tried to keep sex under wraps? We ended up with decades of repression, hairy knuckles and entirely too many perverted Catholic priests. So why should we make the same mistake with shit?

I mean … when babies poop "baby poop," Mommy says "That's kaka!" "That's dirty!" "Don't touch that shit!" And from the earliest days of our lives we are taught that shit is bad and we should avoid getting near it at all times. Except, of course, when we shit, and then there is little choice in the matter.[1]

The vast majority of humanity says "Shit!" They say it a collective 76.9 billion times per day (www.beeblebroxitis.com/stats/shit.html) and take a shit 9.665 trillion times a year. And at an average of 7.6 ounces per defecation, that's 73.45 trillion ounces of human planetary shit per revolution of the earth around Sol.

Seems to me like we should know more about shit and appreciate how much a part of our lives shit really is.

The average American spends 228.125 hours per year shitting, or as some people

OH MY GOD! IT GETS WORSE WITH EACH ORBIT! WHOOOEEE!

---

1 But then again, I did have this one friend who upon exiting the bathroom in a terrific sweat would exclaim, "I am allergic to my own shit!" I never saw any of his allergic test results, but shitting did seem to take a lot out of him.

with constipative relief might say, "2.6 percent of my life is spent on the toilet grunting and going 'ahhhhhhhh.'"

Shit is a ridiculously flexible word and is perhaps the only English language word that can be used as *any* part of speech, *including* a gerund.

Gerunds? Huh?

Gerund: The shittiest part of speech in the English language.

No one knows what a gerund is, unless they learned it in the 1920s. Or went to my parochial grade school.

Recognize a shitty gerund when you see one.

Every gerund, without exception, ends in -ing. Gerunds are not, however, all that easy to pick out. The problem is that all present participles also end in -ing. So, what is the difference?

Gerunds are verb forms that function as nouns. Thus, gerunds will be subjects, subject complements, direct objects, indirect objects, and objects of prepositions. Present participles, on the other hand, complete progressive verbs or act as modifiers. Read these examples:

Since Dennis was five years old, *shitting* has been his passion.

Shitting = subject of the verb *has been*

Dennis' first love is *shitting*.

Shitting = subject complement of the verb *is*

Dennis enjoys *shitting* more than spending time with his girlfriend Susan.

Shitting = direct object of the verb *enjoys*

Dennis gives *shitting* all his energy and time.

Shitting = indirect object of the verb *gives*

When Dennis brought Charmin to class, everyone knew that he was devoted to *shitting.*

Shitting = object of the preposition *to*

One day last summer Dennis and his coach were *shitting* at Daytona Beach.

Shitting = present participle completing the past progressive verb *were shitting*

A great white shark ate Dennis' *shitting* coach.

Shitting = present participle modifying *coach*

Now Dennis practices his sport in safe *shitting* pools.

Shitting = present participle modifying *pools*[2]

Enjoy shit, and learn how to use shit in any situation … correctly, without fear of embarrassment.

What is poop made of?

About three-fourths of your average turd is made of water. Of course, this value is highly variable – the water content of diarrhea is much higher, and the amount of water in poop that has been retained (voluntarily or otherwise) is lower. Water is absorbed out of fecal material as it passes through the intestine, so the longer a turd resides inside before emerging, the drier it will be.

2 http://chompchomp2.com/gbfree/terms/gerund.html provided the original version of this explanation, but they used a different verb, of course.

Of the remaining portion of the turd, about one-third is composed of dead bacteria. These microcorpses come from the intestinal garden of microorganisms that assist us in the digestion of our food. Another one-third of the turd mass is made of stuff that we find indigestible, like cellulose, for instance. This indigestible material is called fiber, and is useful in getting the turd to move along through the intestine, perhaps because it provides traction. The remaining portion of the turd is a mixture of fats such as cholesterol, inorganic salts like phosphates, live bacteria, dead cells and mucus from the lining of the intestine, and protein.

Why does poop stink?

Poop stinks as a result of the products of bacterial action. Bacteria produce smelly, sulfur- or nitrogen-rich organic compounds such as indole, skatole, and mercaptans, and the organic gas hydrogen sulfide. These are the same compounds that give fats their odor.

Why is poop brown?

The color comes mainly from bilirubin, a pigment that arises from the breakdown of red blood cells in the liver and bone marrow. The actual metabolic pathway of bilirubin and its byproducts in the body is very complicated, so we will simply say that a lot of it ends up in the intestine, where it is further modified by bacterial action. But the color itself comes from iron. Iron in hemaglobin in red blood cells gives blood its red color, and iron in the waste product bilirubin gives rise to its brown color.

Now you know your shit.

Grammar and the Shitty Parts of Speech

... IT'S JUST THE SHIT YOU GO THROUGH EVERY DAY. ALL THE DAILY COMPANY SHIT, THE CLIENT SHIT I PUT UP WITH, THE SHIT REPORTS, THE LUNCH MEETING SHIT, COMPUTER UPGRADE SHIT, COMPANY POLITICS SHIT... I JUST WISH THE DAILY SHIT WAS MORE PREDICTABLE! OH SHIT! THAT JUST REMINDED ME... GO AHEAD AND READ THE NEXT COUPLE OF PAGES WHILE I GO AND TAKE MY MORNING SHIT...

Shit is the most flexible word in the English language, bar none. Properly used, and with enough tutelage, shit can account for up to 7.5 percent of everyday speech. Making use of shit's finer nuances in conversation will make communication and clarification far easier than it is today. Relegating shit to the lexicographic and syntactic junk heap is an insane overreaction to political correctness.

Undisputable Fact:

Shit is the only word in the English language that can instantly turn any noun in the English language into an adjective.[1] I know this seems beyond reason, but so does quantum mechanics. This gives a fluent shitty English speaker incredible power, flexibility, and creativity in communication of any sort.

Computer Shit: Technical term referring to anything that has to do with computers. Shit is the noun being modified by Computer, which functions as an adjective.

Party Shit: The old box in the garage that contains the hats, noisemakers, confetti, and disco ball.

MARTHAAAA! WHO PUT THE DRIED-UP TURD IN THE PARTY SHIT BOX?

OOOH BOY...

Party Shit

1 For the grammatically challenged, an adjective modifies a noun: The shitty (adj.) dinner (noun). He (pronoun) was a shitty (adj.) dresser.

Couch-Shit, Car-Shit, Techno-Shit: Very much like the suffix-gate came into vogue after Watergate, 'shit' is also a valuable catch-all phrase that means loosely translated, "all of the et ceteras, et als, and so ons, about a particular object, person, action or event". See how flexible "shit" can be?

Shitty Syntax

Here are examples of how shit can be used anywhere and anytime, and in almost any context. Read on ...

Noun: Shit (Speaks for itself)

Pronoun: Shit, 3rd person personal. In some areas, he-she-it, are used as three third person pronouns, but with increasing feminist political clout, he-shit are now the only two politically correct forms.

Verb: I shit   You shit   He/She/It shits   We shit   You shit   They shit

Past: I/You/He Shat   I have shit   I had shat ('I had shit' uses shit as a noun, so is a blatantly wrong verb form)

Future: I/You/He will shit

Conditional: I could have shit or I could have shat.   I would have shit or I would have shat.   I should have shit or I should have shat.

Adverb: Shittily

Participle: I was shitting (verb plus "ing")

Gerund: Shitting alone is no fun   (noun plus "ing")

Infinitive: To shit   To have shit   To have shat   Having been shit upon so many times …   To have been shitting that much means …

Preposition: Using shit as a preposition is a comparatively modern trend in shitifying the English language. Its use is sparse, but gaining popularity, primarily in the Northeast United States and Puddletown, United Kingdom.
In shit of = in back of (Alternate meanings are = in case of, or = in spite of) By shit of = by way of (Shitting to Joe = according to Joe) Shit for = except for (Joe got all the marbles and shit for the blue ones)

Conjunction: "Bob, shit! Sheila, shit! Their kids are coming to dinner." (Rare usage, generally heard when one is unsuccessfully performing a frustrating task, being beaten around the head with a bat, or burning one's hands in boiling water.)

Interjection: Shit!

Vowels, Syllables: Shit! (one syllable. Northeast, California)

Sheee-ut! (Two syllables. Same regions as additional expressiveness as well as used in the more rural areas)

Sheeeeeeeeet! (One syllable said for three long vowel lengths)

Shee-uh-i-eet! (Four syllables, as said in portions of Idaho, West Virginia and Miami)

Prefix: Shit-heel, Shitload. Shit-hammer. (While the use of the hyphen is not necessarily required from a punctuation standpoint, it does make readability of this shit form much easier. Some experts also suggest that shitty prefixes can be represented by words: shitload. My opinion is that it doesn't matter as long as you pronounce shit and spell shit correctly. You will make your point.

Suffix: (… and shit). All the leftovers and shit. The books and shit in the library. The RAM, CPU, and shit in the computer.

HOly Shit!

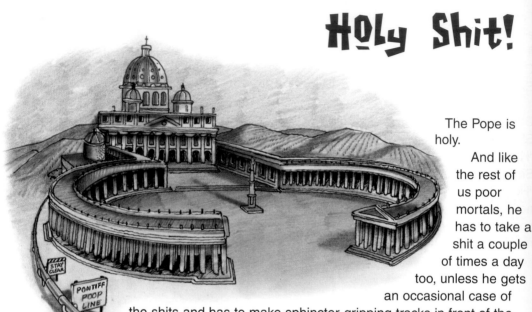

The Pope is holy.

And like the rest of us poor mortals, he has to take a shit a couple of times a day too, unless he gets an occasional case of the shits and has to make sphincter-gripping tracks in front of the *Pieta* on an hourly basis. Nothing wrong with a shitting Pope, eh? But where? When the Pope shits, he sits on the Holy Seat (Where else would he sit and shit?) and the Holy Shit is collected in the basement of the Vatican for subsequent vineyard fertilization. The Holy See is the Catholic government. Get the obvious connection?[1]

---

1 Even Catholics are often confused about the difference between the Holy See and the Holy Seat. The term *Holy See* did indeed originally mean Holy Seat. (Latin: Sancta Sedes, lit, "Holy Seat") http://en.wikipedia.org/wiki/Holy_See

As a good exclamation in polite company, Holy Shit! is usually reserved for awesome (good or bad) things.[2] For example, the only legally acceptable phrase when one first visits the Grand Canyon is "Holy Shit!"

The Hope Diamond. "Holy Shit!" A tsunami. "Holy Shit!" The Sistine Chapel. "Holy Shit!". (No, ees not here señor. It ees collected in the basement. Second door on your left, señor.)[3]

2 Lower classes of society tend to use Holy Shit! entirely too often for my taste. I don't believe an exploding ketchup container at MacDonald's warrants a "Holy Shit!"
3 Eight percent of the Catholic Church's budget is spent on FedEx and other carriers shipping wine (Christ's blood) to diocese around the world. Holy Shit!

More Religious Shit[1]

TAOISM:
Shit happens.

CONFUCIANISM:
Confucius say, "Shit happens."

ZEN:
(What is the sound of shit happening)

JESUITISM:
If shit happens when nobody is watching, is it really shit?

ISLAM:
Shit happens if it is the will of Allah.

COMMUNISM:
Equal shit happens to all people.

PSYCHOANALYSIS:
Shit happens because of your toilet training.

SCIENTOLOGY:
Shit happens if you are on our shit list.

ZOROASTRIANISM:
Bad shit happens, and good shit happens.

UNITARIANISM:
Maybe shit happens. Let's have coffee and doughnuts.

RIGHT-WING PROTESTANTISM:
Let this shit happen to someone else.

JUDAISM:
Why does shit always happen to us?

REFORM JUDAISM:
Got any Kaopectate?

MYSTICISM:
What weird shit!

AGNOSTICISM:
What is this shit?

1 Holy Shit You Can Buy: **www.rubberrun.net/holyshit.html**

ATHEISM:
I don't believe this shit!

NIHILISM:
Who needs this shit?

AZTEC:
Cut out this shit!

QUAKER:
Let's not fight over this shit.

FORTEANISM:
No shit?

12-STEP:
I am powerless to cut the shit.

VOODOO:
Hey, that shit looks like you!

NEW AGE:
Visualize shit not happening.

CATHOLICISM:
Shit happens because you are bad!

DEISM:
Shit just happens.

EXISTENTIALISM:
Shit doesn't happen, shit is.

SECULAR HUMANISM:
Shit evolves.

CHRISTIAN SCIENCE:
Shit is in your mind.

BUDDHISM:
Shit happens, but pay no mind.

SHINTOISM:
Shit is everywhere.

HINDUISM:
This shit has happened before.

WICCA:
Mix this shit together and make it happen!

HASIDISM:
Shit never happens the same way twice.

THEOSOPHY:
You don't know half the shit that happens.

DIANETICS:
Your mother gave you shit before you were born.

SEVENTH-DAY ADVENTIST:
No shit on Saturdays.

JEHOVAH'S WITNESSES:
No shit happens until Armageddon.

HOPI:
Corn fertilizer happens.

MOONIES:
Only happy shit really happens.

BAHA'I:
It's all the same shit.

STOICISM:
This shit is good for me.

OBJECTIVISM:
Our shit is good for you.

...IT'S A HAPPY SHIT, IT'S A HAPPY SHIT, IT'S A HAPPY SHIT, IT'S A...

EST:
If my shit bothers you, that's your fault.

REAGANISM:
Don't move. The shit will trickle down.

FASCISM:
Shit makes the trains run on time.

CARGO CULT:
A barge will come and take all the shit away.

EMACS:
Hold down Control-Meta-Shit.

DISCORDIANISM:
Some funny shit happened to me today.

RASTAFARIANISM:
Let's smoke this shit.

CHARISMATIC:
This is not shit and it doesn't smell bad.

WINDOWS:
Oh shit, re-boot.

This Page Intentionally Left Blank for Your Shit.

Adjectives

Full of shit

One of the most often used phrases across all American cultures. In the U.K. they say bollix or shite. Full of shit is American – as we are often accused of anyway. (No politics.)

Happy as a pig in shit

Even my Southern in-laws and outlaws can't tell me where this came from. If I think of Arnold from "Green Acres," he was always clean. Porky Pig never had soiled trousers.

But it does turn out that pigs can't sweat, so they do like to roll around in cool mud, which acts as the pigskin air conditioning system. Since most shit worth rolling is of the soft variety, it would more than likely have to be warm, thereby not effectively lowering the pig's body temperature. Seems to me that a pig would have no reason to be happy if he was rolling in shit and it made him feel like he had a fever.

Hot shit

Body temperature: 98.6F on average.
Normal Shit temperature: 104.5F on average.
Jalapeño Shit temperature: 105.8F on average.
So, if you are Hot Shit you have Latin blood in you.

Shit brown

About four percent of women and a whopping
25 percent of men are color blind to some
degree or another. I am one of those. So my
tastes in clothes and decorating often leave a
great deal to be desired. I don't hear "You
dress like shit!" only because my
wife puts letters and numbers on my clothes so
I can match them, which are all some
variation on black.

But there is one color anyone,
even a person who only sees shades
of gray, can identify at fifty paces or
one strong whiff: shit brown.

Every local diner or suburban
family restaurant has at least one
dish that looks like shit brown. You
know it. Chile with the thick boiled
scum layer, certain Czech sausages
that ooze in the darndest places or
mashed potatoes and gravy
smeared across the toddler tray. It's
nature.

Then there is yesterday's café-au-lait, jolted with a dash of today's espresso; it's eminently drinkable, but it is, without a doubt, shit brown, and if you keep your eyes open when you sip, you can't help but think sewer.

My favorite shades of shit brown include Mobile Station bathroom curtains and 7/11 condom dispensers. When my best friend spent $38,000 on lifetime aluminum siding for his house, his wife chose her Aunt Ethel's shit brown afghan. Time to move.

Serious shit

(1) You can take a serious shit or a healthy shit and it feels great, doesn't it? Second greatest feeling and all. "Man, I just took a serious shit!" Intense, voluminous, odorous, shartish, relief filled, painful, orgasmic. Take your pick.

(2) "Man, this is some serious shit!" Drugs.

(3) "Man, you into some serious shit!" Crimes. Lawyers, mergers, acquisitions, and business practices of dubious legality. Watergate was some serious shit. Whistleblowers disclose serious shit. Sex in the oval office is stupid but, became serious shit. Serious shit = super intense. (Notice the sexism associated with Serious Shit.)

Serious as shit

This makes no sense, yet kids use it all the time. I would prefer that in grades 1-4, kids are taught that this phrase is just unacceptable.

Shit faced (shiffaced)

By drinking vast quantities of alcohol, one can quickly acquire a shit eating grin, which is what we really mean by shit faced. However these functions are not commutative.[1] Therefore one can become shit faced without having a shit eating grin.

---

1 Math shit. See www.math,com

Shitty

The English language's most often used adjective to describe something of distaste or dislike. A shitty attitude. Shitty weather. Shitty book. In computerese they call this SHITTY*.*

Shitty beer

Warm Mexican any cerveza. Budweiser, any temperature. That Belgian monk crap. Hickory Smoked is the absolute shittiest.

Shitty food

Tongue. Rutabaga. Pork tartare. Deer penis. Most food on Fear Factor.

Shitload

Archaic: The volumetric unit of measure for Chamber Pots and subsequently the first toilets developed by Mr. Crapper. (12 shitloads meant a full case of chamber pots.)

Modern: A whole lot.

"That's a shitload of money."

"You're in a shitload of trouble."

"You're just a shit."

Shitty music

Gangsta rap. Everything else is at least tolerable. Even the occasional German epic opera.

Usual shit

(1) Your common garden variety.
(2) Al Bundy off to the shitter with the sports section folded under his arm.
(3) As opposed to an unusual shit that causes particular pain, contains all of the colors of the rainbow, or forces the shitter (the person shitting) to merrily belt out the words to any Village People song.

Nouns

Free shit

Everyone likes free shit, but we know most free shit is shit. Exhibitors and promotion companies endlessly give out free shit, which often just gets shit-canned when the attendees get to the airport because TSA won't let you take that shit onto a plane. (What a crock of shit that is!)

Once in a while people give out cool free shit, but don't count on it. When I bought my new Mac, Apple gave me a lot of free shit and a 30 percent discount on the other shit I bought.

In London, there is no such thing as Free Shit. At Victoria Station, a shit cost 20p, or about 40 cents. Ain't that the shits?

Is shit stuff? Is stuff shit?

George Carlin has this great rant about Stuff. His live version is about Shit. "Take some stuff on vacation." "Take some shit on vacation?"

In my humble opinion, Stuff is the G-Rated version of Shit. Which is why I totally advocate teaching the proper use of the word shit starting in Kindergarten.[1]

Kung Fu Shit

"You ain't gonna try any of that kung-fu shit on me, Charlie Chan." Chris Tucker to Jackie Chan.

Shit hole

(1) Scatalogists often refer to the cavity that views the water in a toilet as a shit hole. I don't like that. Too gross.

(2) A latrine certainly qualifies as shit hole, as would any hole you shit in for lack of a better equipped facility.

(3) If you have ever had the occasion to visit the WC in some of the less-refined restaurants in Paris, the so-called Turkish toilet is a true shit hole; standing, leaning against a grime-infested wall with your two feet positioned in the concrete indentation. And it's unisex.

(4) Everyone knows someone who lives in a shit hole. A West Virginia trailer park; the bachelor pad roaches voted #1 Dining Experience; the backyard with eleveneen burnt-out car bodies. You know a shit hole when you see one. Back up, don't touch and sterilize!

---

1 I mean, who would say "Take a stuff," "Give a stuff" or "He's a real stuff-heel!" Teach Shit To Your Children Well.

Shit List

Nixon had a shit list. For public consumption, the White House referred to it as the "Enemies List." Getting on someone's shit list can be either a good thing or a bad thing, depending upon your point of view.

After incredible turbulence on a recent flight across the country, the flight attendants had to create a shit list to control the mad panic to the shit hole at the rear.

Shit-talk (Talk shit)

Connotes bragging or exaggeration.

Shit that sucks. (That shit sucks)

- Indian atonal music caused by oxygen deprivation.
- War.
- Your politics. (Not mine.)
- The public school system.
- Anything you like that I don't.

Weird ass shit

"They're dead human bodies," Clements insisted. "Between this heat and all the rain we had a few weeks ago – they get that way. I've seen 'em. They're not some monsters that Hildreth brought here from some satanic sacrifice. The two of you are letting his whole Lucifer-worshipping guru shit bend your brains."[2]

2 p. 328 *Flesh Gothic* by Edward Lee, Dorchester Publishing, 2005, NY. ISBN: 0-8439-5412-4

This Page Intentionally Left Blank For Your Shit.

Actions

Attracts like flies on shit

"He attracts girls at a bar like flies on shit," is actually a compliment. There is no pejorative comparison about women intended.

"He attracts money like flies on shit," is somewhat less a compliment than an observation of fact with some retentive resentment. The comparative value of flies and money are double edged.

"He attracts fat broads like flies on shit," is an insult to the balding fat guy with acne scars and a perpetual Levi jeans wedgie.

This phrase is very easy to misuse and actually can communicate the exact opposite of what was intended. Thus it should only be used by advanced shit speakers.

Beat the livin' shit out of you

Living shit is far better than dead shit, especially if you are the shit container.

This expression comes from the somewhat barbaric games played in medieval England. Along with jousting, a pugilistic game called shite-bounder was played for vast cheering crowds. The object was to beat and subsequently punish your opponent severely enough for him to take a shit or have a major shart on the gladiator's pedestal. The trick though was how to cause him to shit without knocking him unconscious.

The game remained popular in rural Great Britain and still thrived into the 1840s, brought to New York by the Fighting Irish.

Can't cook (for) shit

Heated shit really smells like shit. Ever been to New York in August when the street sweepers are on strike? So putting shit in the microwave is not recommended.

But if you put what was once food into the microwave or oven, and it comes out smelling like shit, then you obviously can't cook for shit.

If you can't cook shit, you are one step below not being able to cook for shit. No chance of anything you cook ever coming out like anything but shit.

I had a British friend who would boil a perfectly good roast beef in brine for four hours prior to serving it. But we all know the Brits can't cook for shit.

Check that shit out

Checking out shit rarely has to do with toilets, circus animals, or diapers. It's more commonly used to refer to a remarkably beautiful woman, an unremarkable oversized woman, or an unexpected and surprising event.

Dipped in shit (warm or otherwise)

"I'll be dipped in shit" was first used by Tennessee mountain people at the turn of the 20th century to acknowledge surprise. Oddly, when heating supplies were low, these same people (large populations of whom all looked alike) would get dipped in shit to add a layer of warmth in the cold winter months.

OH, PEEE-YOOO! MABE ME NOT THAT COLD AFTER ALL!

SHIT WARMING TUB

Fall into warm shit

The accomplished shit aficionado knows that falling into warm shit is far superior to falling into deep shit, from which there is no escape.

Falling into warm shit has its origins from the northern climes of Europe. The Aleuts and other cold weather cultures often measured the temperature by measuring the

DANG! IT JUST SEEMS LIKE I FORGOT TO DO SOMETHING THIS MORNING!

warmth emanating from dogs: "One dog night" is chilly, "Two dog night" is colder and so on. When it got so cold that dog heat was insufficient, some brave soul named Bob discovered that if he lay in the canine latrine, he could stay quite toasty.

Thus falling into warm shit evolved into its current luck-related connotation.

Forget shit

Shit can mean anything as long as you forgot it. Irony is the shits, isn't it?

But, forgetting to shit can also cause the shittiest case of the shits (or sharts) you will ever experience. Govern yourself accordingly.

Get (one's) shit together

Mixing all of the colors of partially hardened Play Dough is the perfect example of kindergartners getting their shit together. Later in life, it's pretty much the same: Quit being a dumb shit.

Go ape shit

See: ANIMALS

Got shit to do.

Grammaticians call this an "actionable noun." Unlike a gerund or participle, which implies current action, "got shit to do" refers to actions in the future. "I can't go bowling cause I got shit to do around the house." (Honey Dos.) "I got some shit to do downtown." (Go to Kinkos, catch up on work at the office, rent a hotel room for 39 minutes.)

(Don't) Know shit

A dumb shit + his knowledge base on any subject at all.

Lose shit

Losing shit is the modern equivalent of, and just as accurate as, "the dog ate my homework."

This is especially applicable in grade schools, where teachers are highly attuned to, and fed up with, lame excuses. Therefore "I lost my shit" is an acceptable catch-all to communicate that the things you were to hand in to the teacher, were part of the "greater shit" and the "greater shit carrier" that was lost.

"I am forever losing my shit."

"You are always losing shit."

The Human Genome Project[1] has concrete evidence that "losing shit" becomes an integral part of vocabulary for those over fifty or for those with an IQ greater than 150.

Shit down your neck

Mafioso threat, circa 1934.[2] This was not a primary concern for those on the receiving end of this threat. The prelude to shitting down your neck was decapitation, a far worse fate to suffer.

1 www.genome.gov/
2 www.americanmafia.com/

Shit on somebody

Well, there are pretty weird as shit people out there, and some of them actually get off on this.

For the rest of us, our bosses shit on us when we do dumb shit. Or, if you're a shit heel, you shit on people because you're just a shit. Not nice.

Shit rains (down) on

Warm shit only rains on lucky people. (See: *Falls into warm shit.*)

Ergo, since when shit rains (down) on someone, it causes grief, heartache, and troubles, it must be cold or frozen shit. If you know the derivation of this, please let me know.

Shit will come down

Shit coming down on you is just short of shit raining on you, unless the shit coming down on you is inside of a piano, which is coincidentally coming down on you with gravity doing its thing. In which case, shit raining on you or a shit storm is far preferable.

Shit your pants

First time it happened to me, I was ten. I was at the bottom of the steep hill to our country house. I ran and ran and pinched my butt cheeks; I made it inside, I saw the toilet, and … (see: *Sharts*)

Today, shit your pants means a total state of surprise. "He shit his pants when he discovered the hard way that 'she' was really a 'he'!" (Lola, the Kinks. 1970)

Proper English also permits 'Shit your pants' to mean an abject state of fear. "He shit his pants when he fell off the bungee platform."

Shoot the shit

In the Old American West, they didn't have a whole lot of Coke cans, plastic milk jugs, or inner city drug dealers. This made target practice somewhat difficult.

So, as an inventive bunch, shit collectors collected cow shit and horse shit and molded it into various shapes to use as targets. Sitting the warm forms in the sun for a few days hardened them so that when shot, they would explode.[3]

"Let's go shoot the shit" meant exactly that. Shooting the shit was made illegal in 1993 with strong support from the Environmental Protection Agency. They maintained – with some significant proof – that shooting the shit caused airborne transmission of disease that could infect humans.

---

3 Shit hitting the fan does not apply since this was before electrification of the West.

Smoke shit
See DRUGS

Talk shit
Lie. Exaggerate. Bullshit.

Turns to shit
In Genesis 19, contrary to the modern translation, Lot's wife did not turn into a pillar of salt when she looked back at the UFOs wreaking havoc upon Sodom and Gomorrah. She was actually scared shitless by seeing round flying machines particle beaming the shit out of two fairly large metropolitan areas.

The most recent translations from the original ancient documents[4] suggest that 'turning to shit' was a direct historical reference to the destruction of Sodom and Gomorrah.

Walk into warm shit
Walking, falling, raining? Whatever. You are a lucky shit heel.

[4] http://mb-soft.com/believe/txs/genesis.htm

EmOtiOns

Guilty as shit

A shit-eating grin is a pretty good clue that someone is guilty as shit. Look for brown crud in their teeth, too. Another clue.

Scared shitless (Scare the shit out of____)

When a condemned man (or Anne Boleyn) sees the steps of the gallows (or the neck rest on a tree stump), it's either complete faith in an afterlife or getting scared shitless. A dangling broken neck is the Old West's recipe for fertilizing the town square and where the term "human waste" came from.

So, it came to be that if you were scared shitless before you were hung, Texas law put you back into the cell for the night, but there was no second last feast.

GERONIM... (ULP!) SHIIIIIIIT!

Shit your pants

My first and only bungee jump. It was just in my mind – a fantastically impossible dream … and I still shit my pants.

Shits and grins

If you do something for shits and grins, you do it just because it's fun. There may be no compelling reason other than pure capriciousness, greed, or hedonism.

Shits and grins became associated with each other thousands of years ago when men and women grimaced while taking a particularly difficult and presumably painful shit. The Greeks called it 'skata eureka,' which loosely translated means "Eureka! I just took a great shit!"

The Eureka! smile and an "it hurts like shit" grimace are often confused, lending the dual meaning.

Shits and giggles

Shits and grins for the gay community. Just picture Pee Wee Herman taking a shit and being amused by it.

Exclamations

Shit!

Smash your finger with a hammer. "Shit!" comes right out of your mouth. Instantaneously.

You lose a big deal at work. "Shit!" says your boss ... and so do you.

There is no more used single syllable exclamation than "Shit!"[1]

"Shit!" is an exclamation of anger, frustration, pain (not good pain, bad pain, but that's another story). Say it. Scream it ... NOW! You will discover the power of "Shit!" in seconds. Trust me on this. It works for me.

Oh, shit!

It turns out, and I didn't know this until January 2005, that 78 percent of people who face imminent, violent and unexpected death shout "Oh, shit!" an average of 4,589 milliseconds before they meet their Maker.

Ohhhh shit.

None the less, "Oh shit!" is quite a distinct exclamation from mere "Shit."[2]

Rather than the anger associated with "Shit!" ... "Oh, shit!" is more of a resignation of fate. As the piano hurtles from the roof toward your head, and there is no escape ... "Oh, shit."

"Oh, shit" can be said with melancholy if your aunt dies or with personal exasperation if you forgot to turn off the stove and realized it after taking off for Europe.

---

1 No shit! Wickipedia covers this quite completely. It is estimated that the word Shit is uttered approximately 23.8 billion times per day in all languages.

2 Or when Windows crashes. This alone is responsible for over 1 billion Shitty utterances per day.

Aw, shit!

"Oh, shit!" Southern style.

O' shit!

Leave it to the Irish! The O' Shit clan can be traced back to the village of Shitternaught in 1452.[3] The O' Shits immigrated to New York City in the early 1820s, but were forced to change their name to O' Shea. No shit! Check it out yourself.

No shit

It happens to all of us. We get the urge, sit down and nothing happens. No shit. A quick perfunctory wipe and back to preparing dinner.

When I grew up, saying "No shit!" was taboo, and we had to say, "No way!" or "You liar!" and with my kids, the perennial "Duh!" sufficed for school hallways.

Alternate Meaning: In distinction to "Duh!", no shit also means, depending upon the situation, "You have to be kidding me?!?"[4] I consider these to be valuable examples.

"I just won the lottery!" No shit?

"The fungus on my toes is so bad the doctor has to amputate at the ankle." No shit?

"Brad and Jen broke up?" So what.

No (participle) shit

As you learned earlier, a participle is a noun that ends in -ing and helps to turn a noun into an adjective. Add the obvious participle or try your own, for example, No walking shit? No bleeping shit? Nah, that shit don't work.

---

3 I, too, am sick of these footnotes, but historical accuracy is important to a shitty author like me. Visit **www.microsoft.com/shit/** for the complete history.

4 "No shit" is an expression of temporary disbelief. Or, maybe permanent, especially if the claims exceed any sense of credulity. For the phrase to work, it must not replace "Bullshit!" as a defiant contradiction. "No shit" implies a portion of belief, in search of further elucidation, explanation, and proof to convince someone you are not bullshitting. "Bullshit" often follows "no shit" when the primary claims/statements are indefensible.

Sheeeeeet!

Sheets are used on beds to protect the mattress from shit leaks. (No shit! Think about it.)

Sheeeet (and the syllabic variables) is used by people who make up beds in hotels when they discover leaked shit.

Shit, Emma

(Like, hell, Emma, "Heckfire, Emma," etc.)

Shit fire!

Add a little punctuation and you have, "Shit! Fire!"

But the origin of the phrase comes not from the hills of Tennessee, but from downtown Nashville, Tenn, itself. On 1st Avenue, right along the Cumberland River, a turd warehouse caught fire in 1877 and it, well, smelled like shit. Duh!

The Tennessean, the local paper, billed the three-day conflagration "Fertilizer Fire on First," but everyone locally called it the Shit Fire. (Think weather and Shit Storm. See? It makes sense.)

In grand Southern tradition, Shit Fire is sorta like Hell Fire, Damn!, Whoa Nellie! to indicate a major event, but probably not a good one.

Shit, yes!

The Beatles song, "You say shit yes, I say shit no …" demonstrates the Liverpool, UK regional use of shit.

COMMON Senses

It's really rather amazing that shit can be used with every human sense. All five (or six) of them. This says something about that scatological fixation we humans apparently have. Just think how many of you take a quick peek to see today's geometric configuration of your shit. Honest, now.[1]

Here goes.

Can't feel shit

If you're in the habit of not using toilet paper, not being able to feel shit will be a tremendous handicap. When your foot falls asleep at the movies, you fall on your face cause you can't feel shit with it. Wait for the credits to roll.

Can't feel for shit

A sociopath's emotional angst.

Can't see shit

Damn it's dark!
A highly effective silk blindfold.
If you can't see shit, how do you know you are done?

Can't see for shit

My eyesight is 20/450. Legally almost blind without Coke bottles strapped to my face. At night, I really can't see for shit at all.

---

1 The correct answer is 43.6 percent of males and 87.1 percent of you girls.

Can't hear shit

Huh?

Can't hear for shit

Turn up the hearing aid, the television, the radio, or your spouse.

Can't smell shit

Truly a benefit in a heatwave during a New York garbage strike.
Truly a handicap if you like Indian or Thai food.

Can't smell for shit

Inhaling quantities of mentholyptus will usually achieve this goal.

Can't taste shit

There is a huge difference between the inability to taste shit or the lack of desire to taste shit. Every baby has tasted shit of course, and my dead dog QBL ate his own shit presumably because he liked the taste of it.

A head cold will totally hose your shit-tasting skills.

Don't listen to that (his/her) shit

Shit can't talk. It can smell, but except for the pharmaceutically challenged, shit won't utter a single word. A squeak or toot perhaps, but no words.

His/Her shit doesn't stink

Most people's shit stinks to high heaven, but there are some notable exceptions: Julia Roberts, Cher (divas, et al), George Clooney and most Members of Congress.

Feels like shit

Having the flu, desperate cold or allergy.

Universal term for hangover.

In a blind touch test, 43 percent of participant could not tell the difference between runny mashed potatoes and fresh cow shit. Really makes me wonder.

Listen to this shit

(1) Some guy is talking shit on TV, the radio, or stage and you call him on it.

(2) Great music!

(3) Shitty music! (See the difference?)

(4) Reading the FDA approved list of carcinogenic ingredients in Big Macs.

(5) The Patriot Act.

Looks like shit

Think about the party where you got shit faced on chocolate martinis with Guinness chasers. You smoked too many Cubanos … and inhaled. You passed out in the hotel in your only good clothes at 4 a.m.

A Guarantee: At the 6:30 breakfast, you will look like shit.

Sounds like shit

Modern digital music sounds like pure, unadulterated shit. Forget the shitty music; I'm talking the quality of the recording. Even my son agrees and gets off on this shit.

Tastes like shit.

Austin Powers II and Fat Bastard's boiling waste product. Some people.

Animals

Bear shit (Does a bear shit in the woods?)

The answer is … sometimes, but not always.

Sometimes bears will shit on the road, a golf course or a parking lot if they can't hold it on the way back to the woods. In Whistler, B.C., Canada, they shit on Whistler Way, coming up from the village past the Westin Hotel.[1]

When they do shit in the woods, black bears shit readily identifiable blackberry shit (or is it blue?) and blue bears (or is it brown bears?) shit black or blue, too. But no matter … the question has been answered.[2]

Bird shit

My wife's car got hit by a plummeting shit from Big Bird[3] the other day. Personally, sea gull and pigeon shits are a minor nuisance[4], but Big Bird shit that lands on a windshield can obliterate the driver's view. The National Traffic Safety Administration estimates that 2,400 accidents annually are caused by Big Bird shit.

1 The Westin maintains a full-time bear shit picker-upper on staff. www.westin.com
2 Source: *The Highlander*, Whistler, B.C., Canada
3 I am personally convinced that Jim Henson, who created *Sesame Street*, was unaware of the damage caused by Big Bird
4 Typically, a 1- to 3-gram splatter over 1- to 4 cm

HMMMM..."LUES ANAMALIUM, QUAE ANGLICE SCITTA VOCATUR, LATINE AUTEM FLUXUS INTERANEORUM DICI POTEST"... THE COWS SHIT THEIR BRAINS OUT ALL OVER THE COUNTRYSIDE...

Not enough car owners know that the active chemical $C_4NH_8O_2$ contained in bird shit will eat through the best auto paint in less than 24 hours, and then begin to eat away at the metal. Corvettes and other cars made from polymers are much less susceptible to bird shit corrison.

Cow shit

They used to call them cow paddies but the Irish Shite Rebellion of 1902 put a quick end to that after a dozen cowboys were smothered in a most horrible way.

Bull shit

Cow shit is an efficient natural fuel source, distributed in the form of a cow patty. Bull shit and bull patties fulfill the same task, but contain up to 400 percent more stored energy. A Bullshit Meter is used to measure the fuel efficiency of any given patty of cow shit or bull shit.

The 1880s was a particularly cold decade due to the global climate change caused by the Southeast Asian volcanic eruption of Krakatoa, and the demand for the more fuel efficient bull shit was in high demand. Fraudulent Bullshit Meters were used to measure higher fuel efficiency and bilk customers out of millions of dollars.[5]

Thus, the derivation of the pejorative term in use today, "Ahhhh bullshit!"

Camel shit

The most prevalent ingredient in French cigarettes.

[5] The size and extent of BSMF, Bullshit Meter Fraud in today's dollars makes the Enron scam minor by comparison.

Chicken shit

Little brown or black pellets that come oozing from the chicken when a chicken is startled, chased by a hen three times its size, or when it sees a geek coming its way.[6] In the expansion of the American West, chickenshit quickly became synonymous with yellow, coward and lily-livered.

Dinosaur shit

When *Jurassic Park* was released in the theatres, children and parents were astounded to discover that dinosaur shit[7] was released in 5,000 to 9,000 kilogram mounds.

Dolphin shit (Aardvark shit, etc.)

These days, all animals shit. Or at least we think so.

YOU KNOW, FOR AS INTELLIGENT AS THEY'RE SUPPOSE TO BE, HE COULD AT LEAST HAVE DROPPED OFF SOME CLEANING TISSUE!

---

6 The term "geek" comes from the Kentucky-Tennessee area in the 1920s, when grandmas and grandpas found it more efficient to bite the head off of a chicken that attempt to hack it off with a machete.

7 Bracchiaraus in this case

Dog shit & cat shit

(1) Household pet feces left for the maid to clean up. **(2)** Household pet feces left by Fido when the family goes away for the weekend and forgets to lock the bedroom door. **(3)** Household pet feces guaranteed to kill the most hardy house plant.

I have not yet found a widespread idiomatic use for either dog or cat shit in any sentence that does not specifically reference dog or cat shit as an object.[8]

Donkey shit

This is how you say "Thank you" to someone in the Schleswig-Holstein area of Germany. The rest of the German population prefers *Danke Shöen*.

Horse shit

There are several words in the English language that are taxonomically categorized as sneeze words. Sneeze words spontaneously erupt from those sneezers who are unable to contain the volume of their sneeze.

The most common sneeze words are Massachusetts, where Chusse- becomes the emphatic sneeze syllable. "Solzhenitsyn,"[9] (Nits-is is the sneeze sound) and horseshit, where sheshi is the sneeze syllable. Pretend to sneeze and try it right now, "Horseshit!"

Sea gull shit

Sea gull shit does not refer to the shit emitted from a sea gull's rectum. In fact, it refers to a corporate manager who employs Seagull Management. In these very common situations where the Peter Principle has been met or exceeded, a manager comes into a meeting, makes a lot of noise, eats all the sandwiches and flies out, leaving shit and confusion everywhere.

---

8 Please let me know if you can elucidate this for my audience.
9 The Russian activist author.

Shit Sue

(1) An inbred breed of Chinese dog with expanded chest and warped smile. (a/k/a Shih Tzu, named after the famous warrior philosopher Sun Tzu)

(2) Johnny Cash said this to the Boy Named Sue.[10]

Hobby Horse shit
(Does a Hobby Horse shit in the nursery?)

Nope. It's your toddler lying to you. Check the DNA. It won't match the hobby horse. Guaranteed.

10 www.toptown.com/hp/66/sue.htm

This Page Intentionally Left Blank For Your Shit.

People

Dip shit

From 1347 to 1352, the highly contagious Black Death killed one-third of Europe's population. Food was scarce in urban areas so village people took to animal (and occasionally human) shit eating as a means of sustenance. It was the French however, who made the practice somewhat less repulsive by rolling the portions in crumbs, sawdust and then deep frying them in available boiling oil concoctions. By dipping the shit into the boiling

shit cauldron for a full minute, the majority of the bacteria was killed off.[1]

Today, a dip shit is someone of foolish quality who acts in an asinine, rude or offensive manner. Linguists disagree on how direct a relationship there is between the

---

1 It should be kept in mind that around this same time in history, the French reinvigorated their interest in perfume, which is believed to have also been used to ameliorate the concurrent smoldering odor.

English dip shit and the French *baisse merde*, or BM, which, by the way, is how Bowel Movement evolved.

We know that the future of dip shit is assured. Its use in the year 2286 proves the term's innate long term-value.[2]

Dumb shit

A dumb shit might be a dip shit, but there is near 100 percent certainty that a dip shit is a dumb shit. If you are that dippy, you have to be pretty dumb.

Jack shit

Native of Edinburgh, Scotland (b. 1613, d. 1697) Mr. Shit was the dominating entrepreneur in sheep patty manufacture and distribution in the Scottish home heating industry.

During the Manure Mania in 1649, the magnesium content of local farm animals was reduced by up to 27 percent for almost three decades.

Mr. Shit, whose family had commerced in shit since the 800s, was one of the fortunate few farmers whose flocks were not afflicted by the still unidentified disease. Thus shit for a heating source was priced at a premium, but still less than wood.

Jack Shit largely controlled the manure-based heating market, but his idiosyncrasies caused him to only do business with people he knew. Thus, when those in search of his essential product would attempt to gain his attention, his business associates would tell them, "Sorry, you don't know Jack Shit."

---

2 From the script of *Star Trek IV*; The Voyage Home. http://www.geocities.com/ussmunchkin7/Star Trek IV.htm

GILLIAN: "That's not what he said, farm boy. Admiral, if we were to assume these whales are ours to do with as we please, we would be as guilty as those who caused – past tense – their extinction. (pause) I have a photographic memory. I <u>see</u> words." (A Silence)
SPOCK (to KIRK): "Are you sure it isn't time for a colorful metaphor?"
GILLIAN: "You're not one of those guys from the military, are you? Trying to teach whales to retrieve torpedoes, or some dipshit stuff like that?"
KIRK: "No ma'am. No dipshit."
GILLIAN: "Well, that's something. I'da let you off right here."

Hot shit

Yes, fresh shit is inherently warm, and on a cold winter day it will look like it is steaming hot. But the BTU retention factor is fairly low, and hot shit will turn to cold, rock-hard shit in a matter of hours.

So, when a snow boarder (or any other artistic type) is called hot shit, it means that while the performance is smokin,'[3] his esteem may be short lived.

Shit hammer

I went to school with a kid named Shit Hammer .[4] No shit. He wrote in 4 pt. type, tried to beat me up and is now a screaming queen who hangs out in front of Lincoln Center looking for acting jobs.

Little shit

"You little shit!" is what Mr. Wilson actually shouted at Dennis the Menace, but the censorship sensibilities of the 1950s insisted he shouted, "Oh, you!"

The current usage, such as in "the little shit shot me," can mean the little shit is (1) a child, (2) a midget, (3) a person of little regard.

3 Jim Carry, *The Mask*
4 To protect the guilty, I won't use his name, but just translate into German.

Shi'ite

A member of the branch of Islam (25 to 30 percent) who regards Ali and his descendants as the legitimate successors to Muhammad and rejects the first three caliphs. Not to be confused with the British pronunciation of shite.

Shit bag

A shit bag is a person who fills a bag with fresh shit from somewhere, lights the bag on fire and puts it on the porch of some poor unsuspecting person's porch. The shit bag rings the doorbell and runs into the bushes in hopes the victim answers barefoot and still tries to stomp out the burning bag.

Shit box

Noun. 1. The anus 2. A contemptible thing, place or person. 3. Shit Eater

Shit head

Being a shithead is far worse than a shitfinger.

Shit heel

A shit heel is decidedly worse than a shit head. A shit head can be downright mean while acting shitty. A shit heel is not only acting shitty but he is traitorous and duplicitous about it, too. A shit head is sort of an evil known quantity, while you really have to be much more on guard around a shit heel.[5]

Shit it in

Leave it to the Aussies for this shitty entry. "Shit it in" means to win a game or sporting event, or to achieve a level of success like getting the cool job instead of the shitty one.

---

5 Get a sheet of paper, make two columns and put past and present personal acquaintances in the appropriate places. The distinction quickly becomes clear.

Shit for brains[6]

I have worked for four companies where the last name of the vice president was "Shitforbrains."

They were Bob Shitforbrains (1978-1981), Al Shitforbrains (1981-1984), David Shitforbrains (1984-1986) and Whattaschmuck Shitforbrains (for three hours in 1989). Amazingly, none of them were related. In 2004, 27.3 percent of management jobs were filled by people whose last name is Shitforbrains or had been changed to Shitforbrains within three months of receiving their MBA.[7]

Shitforbrains also refers to the general group of people who wear aluminum hats to keep the government from reading their minds with the One World Satellites.

---

6 I just want you to think about the last dinner scene in *Hannibal*, and then use your imagination.

7 www.shitforbrains.com

Shit Monster

From the religious "shie-mon" and popularized in Kevin Smith's 1999 religio-historical movie *Dogma*.

Shit tacks

(See Shit a brick) Also: Often mistaken for shiitake (a/k/a shitake) mushrooms used in Asian cuisine. "This here moo goo guy pan has so many shiitakes, it tastes like shit."

Stir the shit (shit stirrer)

My wife thinks I made this shit up just to add another page. Nay, Wench! It must just be a phrase from that small regional shit hole in the Northeast we affectionately call New York!

A shit stirrer

Imagine you are at a party. Bob has had too much too drink and his wife Cordelia (yeah, a real shitty name, but her middle name is Frau Yuch) watches Bob slobber all over big breasted Bambi, who is oblivious to it all. Cordelia slams back two double Jack's and slithers up the hind leg of young six-pack Matt, Bambi's date.

Now the shit hits the fan. Bob goes ballistic on Cordelia. Cordelia accuses Bob of having two affairs in the last year.

You, the shit stirrer, say, "Bob, did you forget the weekend you spent with Carla?" Cordelia throws the glass of Jack on the rocks at Bob.

Bob ducks and shoots back about her one night stand in Cancun on their honeymoon.

Next you say, "Cordelia, was Cancun really your first fivesome?" Bob leaps off of the barstool and tries to choke the living shit out of Cordelia.

It takes two cops, mutual restraining orders and a lot of drunk partygoers talking shit to the cops to calm things down. You are a shit stirrer. You stirred the shit. You had a great evening.

Just for Kicks

Kick the shit out of you

This term is often attributed to "Hangin' judge" Roy Bean, a notoriously drunken, vindictive and reliably crazy Texan justice of the peace in the late 19th century.[1]

When one is hanged, the hangee shits his pants. Can't help it. Your neck goes hither, your neck goes yon, and your sphincter muscle joins the *Great Shit Hole in the Sky*, allowing rapid escape of The Last Meal.

In kinder, more sober moments, Judge Bean let convicted criminals who suffered his "Hang 'em first, try 'em later" mantra choose something other than having one's last act on this earth being shitting one's pants.

"You can hang, or have the shit kicked out of you." Judge Bean's twisted logic was that the criminal would be so embarrassed by having the shit (literally) kicked out of him, he would straighten out.

1 http://www.desertusa.com/mag98/aug/papr/du_roybean.html

Kick the (livin') shit out of you

Reserved exclusively for shit kickings that occur after a meal of oysters, clams, sushi or raw roadkill.

Kick the (ever livin') shit out of you

Only used by low-level mobsters, enforcers and muscle men in Brooklyn, New York, who want to show they can string two two-syllable words together in one sentence.[2]

Shit kicking

(Obs.) A form of justice and humiliation where the contents of one's lower intestines are kicked out of the body onto a public platform in town squares.

(Mod.) A fight where one combatant clearly defeats the other. A shit kicking usually occurs outside of a country music bar, behind the high school gym or in cell block B.

2 See "Dumb Shit"

Shit kicker(s)

The person or persons who do the shit kicking. Can also refer to the U.S. Armed Forces on any given day. Shit kickers generally don't take shit from anyone.

Shit kickers

(Obs.) Cowboy boots, circa 1890, with specially formed toes to make kicking the shit out of someone less damaging to the anus.

Modern usage includes reference to "nose pickers," shoes and boots that have needle-pointed toes. Several creative uses were demonstrated on David Letterman's "Stupid People Tricks" in May 1993.

WHAT ARE YOU LOOKIN' AT?

This Page Intentionally Left Blank for Your Shit.

Give and Take

Catch shit

If shit were the flu, we would all catch it.

If shit were $100 bills, sure as shit, we would all *try* and catch it.

Baseball catchers have to catch the shit pitchers throw at them.

Then, because shit flows downhill, management doesn't catch shit.[1] They make sure their underlings, subordinates and less worthy workers catch all the shit.

If you're a student, just make sure you don't catch any shit from your English teacher for reading this shit.

DON'T GIVE ME ANY OF YOUR SHIT YOUNG MAN!

Don't take shit off of (from) nobody

Sometimes moms do have to take shit off of someone. Like their shitting offspring. But that's what moms do. Yep.

Otherwise taking shit off of a body in the literal sense is pretty disgusting.

This shit, however, is when someone is talking shit. Or bullshit, as the case may be. Don't take it. Don't let someone push your shit around, or tell you what to do. Don't take any abusive shit off the male of the species. Don't let them ever, ever shit on you. Point made.

1 Except from the stockholders. But by then they have shit all over the investors, the public forgot shit, the lawyers have gone ape shit, and what's left of the company ain't worth shit.

Don't give me any (your) shit

See *Don't Take a Shit*. Same thing, except in the affirmative.

A declaratory means to warn someone about not engaging in some future endeavor wherein the result would be giving you shit. You don't want their shit? Tell 'em loud and clear. "Don't give me *your* shit" implies that the shit giver is overly repetitive with his shit-giving (lies, tall tales, argumentativeness, questioning everything), and has become a bloody bore.

Give a shit

Do you give the toilet a shit? Many cultures believe that there is an intensely personal relationship between the Porcelain God and one's shit. Yeah, I know, that's weird as shit – but hey? As long as they don't give me any shit about my beliefs, I won't give them any shit about theirs.

At any rate, to give a shit, or care about something/someone, etc., is a direct descendant of these belief systems.

Give two shits

If you doubly care about something/someone, then one would think you give two shits about it.[2]

Two shits, though, is more closely related to pico-shit or nano-shit. Just a very tiny amount of shit. Therefore, If you give two shits about something, you really don't care about much at all. It ain't worth shit to you.

Of course, if you seriously bow to the Porcelain God, you can train for years and learn how to turn one shit into two shits, four shits, and for the advanced advocee, eight shits.

Not Gonna Take Your Shit

See: *Don't Take Shit off of (from) Nobody* … and … *Don't Give Me any (Your) Shit*.

2 The math is obvious: Give a Shit = give one shit = Care Level X. Therefore, give two shits should equal Care Level 2X. But, it doesn't.

Take a shit

"Take a shit" and "Take shit" might be tough for many non-English-first-language speakers to differentiate. If you hear them mix 'em up, please do not belittle them, even if they are French. Show them the right way.

Taking a shit is a measurement of time. For example, I am cursed with a high-speed shit rail. For me, taking a shit is "I'll be there in two minutes, sweetheart!" For my brother-in-law, taking a shit is a camping expedition: two magazines, a Stephen King novel, the Sports page of our local newspaper, a Coke, pretzels and an extra light bulb.

I have never heard if anyone has ever taken two shits but I suppose if you counted each flush as resetting the clock, it is theoretically possible.

THIS IS BASICALLY YOUR "IT'S GONNA BE A WHILE, SO I'M GONNA CAMP OUT" SHIT!

This Page Intentionally Left Blank For Your Shit.

Phrases and Quotes

Ain't that the shits

Bifurcated meaning, so much like all shit.

"Isn't that the greatest thing you have ever seen?"

"Of all the rotten luck." (When you get five out of the six lottery numbers, losing $37 million in the process.)

Dipped in shit

A body-warming activity originally practiced by the ancient Novaya Zamlya natives. Fifteen minutes of being dipped in shit brings the body temperature up by 10 centigrade. When the practice migrated south to warmer climates, countless people succumbed to severe body overheating, and the phrase came to mean, "you can fool me once …" or "no shit!"

Double dipped in shit

The body temperature rises by 20 centigrade in fifteen minutes if cayenne or jalapenos are added to the dipping shit.

Get your shit together

Runny shit, diarrhea of the mouth – same thing.

Always late for work, gonna lose your job and in complete debt? Get your shit together.

Taking a long trip and you haven't packed? Get your shit together.

Shit is soooo flexible.

How the shit did that happen?

No one really knows how shit happens. Shit just happens and we are all supposed to deal with it like adults, no matter how much shit we have to go through. As a result, no one ever is ever likely to really know how shit happens. Clear? Like I said, no one really knows how or why shit happens.

Shit Fit

Just shy of a true shit hemorrhage. I had two shit fits recently. Dell and Windows are so shitty, I switched to Mac. The next shit fit was at my bank, AmSouth, for screwing with my account, having lousy online security, and a clueless staff that can be social engineered by Cretans.

I didn't do shit! (Why are you mad or arresting me?)

Mooning from a convertible is arguably illegal, but if you do shit while mooning, that shit is just wrong!

If Big Mama yells at Little Leroy, Little Leroy will automatically respond, "I didn't do shit." If the gang member gets caught with a gun, he will tell the police, "I didn't do shit."

"I didn't do shit" is ebonic for Not Guilty.

Know his shit

Even if were a case of life and death, I doubt one person in a million knows his shit. I mean, it all looks so similar; and if it's liquefied, well, tough shit!

But if you do know your shit, then there is a fairly decent chance you might actually be good at your job. I really think airline pilots, anesthesiologists and exotic dancers should – for public safety – should know their shit.

1 The second greatest feeling in the world. Visit any airport restroom and just listen to that shit!

Shit can

The aluminum version of the chamber pot was introduced in 1942 to increase the sanitation of soldiers in World War II. When the Aluminum Company of America (www.alcoa.com) introduced it to the fledgling television audiences of the early 1950s, it failed miserably, and the result was that the entire marketing department was fired – or shit canned as it is now known.

Shit Vicks VapoRub

Go to a Thai (or Indian) restaurant. Order anything. Meat. Fish. Chicken. Veggies. Order it with SL5. Spice Level 5. Sweat off a few pounds while drinking vast quantities of Singha. The cold sores in your mouth are blistering, your throat is striated with cat scratches and your stomach is rumbling with Center of the Earth Magma. Tasty.

The next morning you are awakened by the sandpaper grinding on your hemorrhoids. Then the true agony begins as you shit Vicks VapoRub.

Tough shit

(1) My sixth grade English teacher used to say "Tough Nugies," but we all knew he meant tough shit, but it was tough nugies on him he couldn't say tough shit. Political correctness guidelines in middle school frown on teachers cursing at students.

(2) I talked with a few doctors, but I could not find a consensus on just how tough shit should be. Of course the purity or acidity of the water in your shitter can also affect the perceived toughness (or runniness) of your shit. None of that explains, though, and I could not find out how tough shit came to mean "Bite the bullet," "Learn to live with it," "Life is unfair," "Quit complaining," "Face reality." "So what?"

(3) If you don't understand these definitions, tough shit.

Shit goes down

When the shit goes down the toilet, this is a good thing. Shit going down also refers to a crime or other inappropriate activities in progress.

OK HOLMES, IF YOU NEED THIS SHIT SO MUCH, I'M GONNA GIVE YOU THE REAL DEAL. IF THIS DOESN'T CURE HIM, NOTHING WILL!

No shit, Sherlock.

It's now a historical certainty that Sherlock Holmes was addicted to cocaine.[2]

Awakening from a nap and a long period of "dreamy, vacant expression," Holmes looked for another fix.[3] Dr. Watson had come to realize the addictive and damaging effects of cocaine. He found and removed the hypodermic syringe in its morocco case from the mantle and promptly disposed of it.

2 *The Chronicles of Sir Arthur Conan Doyle.* http://www.siracd.com/work_h_cocaine.shtml

3 Later it became quite clear that Sherlock Holmes was indeed using drugs. "The Sign of Four" opens with an alarming scene: *"Sherlock Holmes took his bottle from the corner of the mantel-piece and his hypodermic syringe from its neat morocco case. With his long, white, nervous fingers he adjusted the delicate needle, and rolled back his left shirt-cuff. For some little time his eyes rested thoughtfully upon the sinewy forearm and wrist all dotted and scarred with innumerable puncture-marks. Finally he thrust the sharp point home, pressed down the tiny piston, and sank back into the velvet-lined arm-chair with a long sigh of satisfaction."* A little later in the story Holmes states, *"It is cocaine," he said, "a seven-per-cent solution. Would you care to try it?"*

When Holmes begged for more of the drug, Watson quietly said, "no shit, Sherlock," which was the first tenuous step in his recovery.

No shit, Sherlock has come to mean, "Duh!"[4]

Same Old shit

My dogs took a shit by our cul-de-sac in Whistler. The next day it was still there, so my dogs spent a couple of minutes sniffing it. The next day they sniffed the same old shit.

Same old shit can be good. Same old shit can be bad. But generally, the same old shit is pretty boring.

Shit Flows downhill

No shit, Sherlock!

Just cause we're talking shit here, doesn't mean the laws of physics have been repealed.

Shit will roll downhill in varying degrees of efficiency. Of course the rounder the shit, the more easily it will counter friction (anti-gravity) and flow/roll downhill. More liquid shit will flow downhill more easily, and that was the great Babylonian contribution to the scatological universe: gravity flow sewage systems.

WHOOOOOAAAAA SHHIIIIIIIIIIIT!

---

4 No shit is roughly the same as No shit, Sherlock, but the addition of Sherlock shows the speaker is new to proper shit speak.
5 Remember, in the old days, villages and towns were often built on hills to make it easier to defend against the enemies who wanted access to their sewage technology.

How simple can we get? Schlepp water to the holding tank on top of a hill.[5] Let the water gently flow down pipes under the streets, and each household feeds its shit (and other bathroom stuff) into the main pipes. The shit flows downhill, and the hillside village smells sweet.

Over the millennia though, sociologically shit became more of a taboo and was associated with bad occurrences or events. When things go awry, especially in Big Business and Government, and the "shit hits the fan," there is a cultural need to blame someone; find a scapegoat or the fall guy. Typically such a person is lower on the corporate ladder, or as many Native American cultures said, "low on the totem pole," or low on the pecking order, using the avian metaphor.

These three fundamentals represent the preferred Western method of dealing with unforeseen events.

Shit depends

1. Presents a generic either/or situation.
2. A phrase used by caregivers at nursing homes, referring to a patient whose incontinence requires that they wear adult diapers.

Shit or get off the pot

From the references to portable shit houses where an occupant is not shitting with enough alacrity and is strongly encouraged to give up his seat to the next person in line.

Common usage, though, is found during board games when one player takes too long to make a move and the other players become annoyed with waiting.

Also increasingly found in corporations and government when an executive is afraid to make a decision in fear for his job. Pretty shitty attitude if you ask me.

Shit from Shinola (Doesn't know the difference)

Shinola was a brand of wax shoe polish available in the early- to mid-20th century. Its immortality in colloquial English comes from its being a dark, sticky semisolid substance distinct from shit.

This distinction inhabits the phrase *"[He] doesn't know shit from Shinola."* Implied is that shit and Shinola are superficially similar in aspect, yet are quite different in value when applied to shoes or carelessly stepped in. One who doesn't know one from the other is therefore critically unwise, inexperienced or of substandard mental ability.

Similar meaning can be found in the expression *"He doesn't know his ass from his elbow."* Retrieved from "http://en.wikipedia.org/wiki/Shinola"

Shit happens

Shit, yes, shit happens. All of the time. Good shit happens, but bad shit happens a lot more than good or even mediocre shit happens. A very workable catch-all for, 'oh, well. What can you do.' Shit happens.[6]

Shit is flying

After the shit hits the fan (see: WEATHER), shit flies in all directions if the fan is oscillating. In all other cases, flying shit tends to flow in the direction of the jet stream. Many American are quite content to know that when shit flies in the jet stream, it drops on France. No shit!

HEY PAL, THAT POLISH SMELLS LIKE SHIT!

IT IS.

SHINEOLA
SHINE
$1.00

---

6 Shit Happens is derived from the Latin actuarial phrase 'Shittus Honumerus," which literally translated is "no one knows the exact figure, so this is our best guess."

That's some good shit. Bad shit.

There is no fundamental difference between good shit and bad shit if, in your particular idiomatic vernacular, you make no difference between good and bad.

Think about pot heads. "This shit is good." They like the cannabis. "This shit is bad." They really, really, like the cannabis. "This shit is bad." Why you making me smoke oregano? (Replace pot with any other shitty noun and the same rules apply.)

SO MUCH FOR YOUR GREAT BUY ON THE SUPER GOLIATH COOLING FAN, HAROLD! AND WHATEVER POSSESSED YOU TO PLACE IT NEXT TO THE KITTY LITTER BOX?

Up Shit's Creek (Paddle)

Shit's Creek is about forty miles from Laramie, Wyoming, although MapQuest won't show it because of threats from the Department of State, Maps Division.[7]

In the 1880s, Jesse James holed up in Shit's Creek, and on May 31, 1892, he was finally captured there by the authorities. *The Laramie Times* announced the following day that James was found "Up Shit's Creek," which is now populated on a full-time basis by all 3.5 billion men on Planet Earth.

7 www.dos.gov

You're shitting me

At a scatology party, this is an invitation or an announcement; either way it is profoundly disturbing. SYN: "No shit?"

I shit you not

Catchphrase coined by Jack Paar, host of the *Tonight Show* from 1957 to 1962. Paar "invented the talk-show format as we know it: the ability to sit down and make small talk big," said Merv Griffin. Paar died on January 27, 2004, at age 85. "Even youngsters sent to bed before Mr. Paar, came on parroted his jaunty catchphrase: 'I shit you not.'" [8]

Beat to shit

Too tired to be believed.
The Boss beats you to shit for doing dumb shit.

(Beat the shit out of)

See: Kick the Shit Out of … except using kitchenware instead of shit kickers.

Reduced to shit

From the software industry: Any operating system that is so appended, added, patched and kludged as to make it a true piece of shit.[9]

---

8 www.jackpaar.com is the official site on shitting people not.
9 http://www.microsoft.com/security/bulletins/default.mspx

This Page Intentionally Left Blank For Your Shit.

Capitalism

Buy into his shit

OK! I'LL TAKE THE THIRD TURD ON THE LEFT!

Purchasing power is everything in a global economy. The object then is to get people to *"buy into your shit"* or *"buy your bullshit"* – meaning, you sold them a bill of goods … you scammed 'em.

"Archie said he got lucky with Veronica. You buy into his shit?"

Here, the word *bullshit* could also be used as a synonymously more derogatory term than mere *lies*.

Buy some shit (K Mart)

The chapter on drugs has its own explanation, but well outside of the dark alley purchases and the manure wholesaler, one can buy shit anywhere.

"I gotta buy some shit at Home Depot (Wal-Mart, Target, etc.)"

Another perfect example of how shit can be anything it wants to be, and everything is shit. Buying shit could mean furnishing the bordello, detailing the car or buying cat shit deodorizers at Pet Smart.

I don't need (want) any of your shit.

(1) The baby-sitter's mantra. Heard over and over again on nanny cams and cell phones every Saturday night.

(2) "Quit lying to me, you dumb shit."

(3) *"Please use someone else's shitter (toilet)."* **We don't want any of your Shit** signs are seen outside of many finer restaurants.

(4) *"Don't you be causing me any of your bullshit/horseshit."* Here, shit is synonymous with "trouble.

(5) Standard phrase that homeowners say to telemarketers and door-to-door salesmen.

Full of Shit[1]

Most diners and *All-You-Can-Eat* places are really full of shit. At the Mongolie Grill in Whistler, BC, Canada, there is a wall of plaques for those die-hard eaters who were able to consume more than 3.8 kg of food at a single seating. They are all full of shit … at least for a while. Then they take a *Mongo Shit* and lose several pounds in the process.

Otherwise, being *Full of Shit* means one is a liar.

"I used to date Demi Moore." You're full of shit.

"I took a ride on an Andovian flying saucer last weekend." You're full of shit.

"I know what I'm talking about." You're *really* full of shit.

URP.., UH... I'M AFRAID THAT URP... THIS DINKY CRAPPER AIN'T GONNA CUT IT...

ALL YOU CAN EAT Champ

Geography

Deep shit (in)

Deep Shit is a quarry pond in Eastern Kentucky, a few miles from Knoblick (No shit!). If you fall from the top edge and survive the plunge, you are in deep shit because there are no beaches or ledges on which to climb.

In *Jurassic Park I*, Laura Dern stuck her entire arm into 4,000 pounds of deep shit excreted by an ailing brontosaurus. Ed Norton, from the 1950s sitcom *The Honeymooners*, spent eight hours a day in deep shit … the New York City sewers.

Deep shit 9

From *Star Trek, the Next Generation*. Deep Shit 9 is a remote space station a few light years from the Neutral Zone.

Do you have any idea how much shit I'm in?

My son said this to a friend on Instant Messenger the other day. We monitor everything he does online because it's our job to keep the little shit out of too much shit. Nonetheless, he

MOM? DAD? I JUST THOUGHT I WOULD BEAT MYSELF TO IT... I'M IN SOME DEEP SHIT!

hadn't handed in a school paper, so his teacher gave him shit … and a letter for me and my wife. So, he knew he was in a pile of shit … definitely knee-deep and precariously close to deep shit.

When asking the question of anyone, you are searching for a quantitively accurate response. "Lots" is not acceptable. "Four pounds," while not a lot of shit, is at least a hard number.[1]

This book will really help you and your family in correctly measuring and communicating the amount of shit one is in, when one finds oneself in shit … of some depth, height, weight or other metric.

Knee-deep in shit

Being knee-deep in shit is not nearly as bad as being in deep shit because most people can crawl out of knee-deep shit … but with effort.

It's sort of like being up to your alligators in asses. May be a tough situation, but it ain't all bad. There is hope.

Where is that shit?

This can mean many things, like: "Where is that little person who acts like a shit?" … or … "Where is the shit that I lost but had in my hands a few seconds ago?" … or … "What did I do with the drugs?"

Since shit can mean any other noun in almost any language, this highly flexible phrase has been rated an astounding 92.3/100 on the English Heritage Context Flexibility Scale.[2]

1 No double entendre was intended, but shit happens.
2 Check in at www.bartleby.com/61/ for updates.

The Weather

Colder/Hotter than shit

How does the thermos know if its contents are hot or cold? A thermos doesn't know shit, so it remains a mystery. The mystery only deepens when shit can be both hot and cold.

In the middle of winter, with the wind blowing, it's colder than shit, which is obvious in large cities because dog shit on the streets is steaming and acting as a heat source.

In the middle of Las Vegas, it is hotter than shit, because the dog shit on the streets doesn't create shit steam. Let it be known that shit is, on average and if truly fresh, just shy of 42 degrees centigrade. No shit!

Flying shit See: Shit Storm

Shit HEMORRHAGE

Imagine getting so incredibly angry that your blood pressure rises to 200/150, the veins on your forehead have become a named mountain range and your ears are fire engine red, engorged to twice their normal size.

You are so angry, your hands are shaking with incredulity. You stammer out sounds and grunts because you cannot articulate the words. Your brain is in a state of total disconnect and your body just might go ahead and do anything it wants because you are no longer in control.

That, my friends, is the onset of a Shit HEMORRHAGE. It only gets worse from there.[1]

---

1 We all know the legal system is the shits, so it should be no surprise that the California courts lead the shit parade. In March 2005, Michael Dilker, 25, was on trial for his life. He had killed his roommate in a fit of rage. His attorney successfully argued, and the jury agreed, that Dilker was innocent due to a predilection to have shit hemorrhages. Mental experts testified that this newly recognized medical condition is on the rise, but is treatable.

Shit Storm

A shit storm is one possible outcome of stirring the shit. It can also occur as one unpredictable outcome of seemingly unrelated events from Chaos Theory.[2]

Oddly enough, shit storms are not all that rare. In the 20th century, more than 500 fertilizer plants in the U.S. alone exploded. This resultant shit can be propelled more than 1 km into the air and, depending upon the winds, the shit can rain down as much as 30 kms away!

When the shit hits the fan

Leonardo da Vinci invented the helicopter at the end of the 15th Century.[3] It really didn't work that well – as in not at all, but not for lack of trying.

Da Vinci designed a spiral wing structure resembling a fan that turned by leg-powered pedals and gears. He knew that hot air rises and that methane gas, the primary released energy from animal shit, was flammable. His genius was developing the basics of the internal combustion engine … 400 years too early. With the limited technology of the day, one couldn't regulate the explosive force of methane gas, air and heat (we call it a carburetor).

For nearly eight years, da Vinci and his team tried hundreds of combinations, but each time there was an explosion of some varying force and the *shit would hit the fan.*

FART HARDER MEN! WE'RE NOT RISING FAST ENOUGH!

Leonardo's HOT GAS-O-COPTER

ALSO: A cocktail containing Kahlua, dark rum, Bailey's Irish Cream and Amaretto.

2 www.imho.com/grae/chaos.html
3 www.bbc.co.uk/historic_figures/da_vinci_leonardo.shtml

Drugs[1]

Bad shit

This purely contextual phrase can be very confusing to non-English-first-language people because bad shit can mean both bad shit and good shit depending upon the intent of the speaker.

Because bad can mean good, and the polysyllabic extended usage of "baaaaaaaaaaaaad" is typical in inner urban areas, often no one has the slightest idea what anyone is talking about.

So, bad shit can mean both good and bad drugs. So simple.

Cut the shit

(1) Dilute the strength of the drugs/cocaine with harmless talc powder or immobilizing horse tranquilizer.

(2) "Now cut that out!"

(3) "Quit lying!"

(4) Pretty flexible, eh?

HEY! THERE'S NO POT IN HERE! THIS IS REAL SHIT! SON, HAVE I EVER TOLD YOU WHATTA GOOD LITTLE SHIT YOU ARE?

Get that shit outta here!

Dad, the narcotics cop in LA, finds a bag of pot in his 17-year-old son's room and says what's on his mind. But sometimes there are surprises.

1 Shit: A morphine derivative (syn: heroin, diacetyl morphine, morphine, "H", horse, junk, scag, smack.) In common usage, marijuana is often referred to as shit, without connoting any hard drug. In part, this is due to the live skunk odor of stronger strains.

Good shit

(1) Whether monosyllabic ("This is some good shit") or polysyllabic ("This is some gooooooooood shit"), good shit can never mean bad shit. So much for drugs.

(2) Every male in the universe knows that taking a good shit is the second best feeling in the world. (With taking off ski boots a close third.)

No officer, no shit in here

"License, registration. You got any of that shit in that glove compartment?"

You smoke that shit?

Just because history blames smoking and related diseases as the Revenge of the Red Man[2] doesn't mean it's true. An oft overlooked, rich Arab history tells us something different. They knew about smoking from trading with China. But tobacco fields were a scarce commodity in Iraq and the Sahara desert, so they had to get creative.

Camel dung was a common source of fuel for heating tents, and papyrus was readily available from reeds. The leap to rolling dried camel shit flakes into papyrus spliffs became quite the rage.[3] Thus begat the phrase *Smoking that Shit*. It is still used when talking about Turkish and Arab cigarettes.

---

2 OK, History buffs. Sir Walter Raleigh, the Brit bringing back tobacco to the UK a few hundred years ago. That's the reference.
3 Attributed to Bob Abdulla, circa 768 CE

Food

Crock of shit

My mom was a single mom, so she put some shit into the crock pot in the morning. By the time I got home from school, dinner was ready. Now *that's* a crock of shit, eh?

Eat shit

Tastes like shit is a big compliment to the chef at a scatological buffet.

Eat shit is also a common response to someone who comes up with a very bad suggestion.

"You go first!" (Dark hole with bugs, into the line of fire, blue food.)

"Eat shit!"

Some freaks are really into serious shit eating. My God![1]

GENTLEMEN, PLEASE DO ME THE COURTESY OF POINTING OUT THE ENTREE THAT SAYS "SHIT" IN THIS MENU!

Eat shit and die

(1) A short story by Cameron Barrett[2]

(2) Not only did you come up with a stupid idea, say something really dumb in public, but your inane actions really caused shit to rain down on me.

---

1 www.thestranger.com/2001-05-31/savage.html. UGH! Do not visit www.theshithole.com. You are seriously warned.
2 www.camworld.com/hiddenfiction/eat.shit.and.die.html

(3) The phrase *eat shit and die* originated in England during the Black Plague[3] for obvious reasons.

Shit eating grin

Yeah, in my research for SHIT I did run across an entire subculture of shit aficionados. Dinner parties must be rough on the dishwashers. But it turns out that a *Shit Eating Grin* is the result of the left brain (which thinks eating shit is cool) trying to convince the right brain (which hates the taste of shit) that the last spoonful was really delicious. The wry, twisted curl of the lips is the result of sensory overload. Man was not meant to eat shit.

Shit on a shingle[4]

During World War II, the US Army had problems getting enough food to the troops on so many fronts. They developed a method that would convert a soldier's personal output into a non-offensive and tasteless edible substance. Soldiers only had to carry a variety of flavor packs which they then added to the MOFO (MObile FOod) units according to their personal taste.

MOFO is generally served on toasted bread, earning it this still popular soldier's moniker.

3 Circa 1348-1351CE. http://history.boisestate.edu/westciv/plague/
4 See: *Tastes Like Shit*

WC

The WC (Water Closet, or room, tent or oasis with a toilet or hole, and maybe a supply of fresh water or sand) is inextricably tied to shit.

The shitter

No surprise here. It's where we shit. Take a look at how many ways you can properly use the shitter in polite conversation. The shitter can mean:

- The toilet itself.
- The hole in the ground in a Turkish prison or at a Four Star French restaurant.
- A latrine.
- The shit house or outhouse. (Note their omnipresence at construction zones, traveling carnivals and outdoor concerts in the steaming humidity.)
- The bathroom itself.
- An airplane lavatory. (Another misnomer. The 'laving' section of the lavatory takes up 83 percent less volume than the shitter itself.)
- Anything else you can shit in.

Hit the shitter

Under rare circumstances it is proper to hit the shitter.[1]

It is certainly permissible if the shitter doesn't behave as it should. If the water fails to drain from the tank over the toilet, one or two small taps will usually solve the problem. Take extreme care when the shitter is made of porcelain. You do not want to go there. Trust me.

---

1 Note: You cannot hit "a" shitter. It must be "the" shitter, even if it is indefinite in location.

You may also hit the shitter when it is miserably cold and pouring, you are standing in a long line for the shitter at an outdoor rock concert or a sporting event and the fool inside the shitter is just taking too long. Hit the shitter and holler, "Hey! You through shitting or what?"[2]

HUFF, PUFF WHEEZE, WHEEZE... SHIT...

Brick shit house

It was all about the Three Little Pigs. "I'll huff and I'll puff and I'll blow your shit house down!" howled the Big Bad Wolf. And as we all know from this fine literary metaphor, the third little pig hid out in the brick shit house and survived. And so this brand name was born.

Today, a brick shit house refers to something extremely well constructed and perhaps over-engineered; built to weather the tests of time and brute force abuse. The Pyramids of Giza are a perfect example of well-thought-out and excessive brick shit house construction.

2 Make sure you step back 8 to 10 paces when performing this particular action.

Shit house

This term originates as far back as early Babylon. Rural villages could not afford to install the latest infrastructures of gravity-flow water, indoor plumbing and sewage control.[3] In an attempt to maintain a modern standard of cleanliness, they chose to erect shit houses, some distance from the living and cooking areas of the home.[4]

Rural areas within the United States commonly used shit houses into the 1960s, renamed "outhouses" as a reaction to American religious sensitivities. Modern usage of shit houses has evolved into a generic term for an abode or other place that has fallen into chaos, filth or other disrepair due to the negligence and lack of hygiene by its occupant.

Due to the current rash of anti-shit movements, parents will not tell their children that their room is a shit house. The more "family-friendly" phrase recommended by most child psychologists is "Your room is a pigsty." And thus, the true heritage of shit house and the Three Little Pigs is reinforced.

Built like a brick shit house

One would be technically correct to say, "The Great Wall of China is built like a brick shit house!" However, it would not accurately reflect the currently accepted nuances of its use.

A subtle transmutation of *built like a brick shit house* began during World War II, European Theater. Because soldiers lived in bivouacs and only had access to outdoor latrines for months at a time, they longed for proper facilities … just about as much as they longed for the company of a woman.

---

3 The 3,500-year-old Palace of Knossos, 4 kms outside of the capital of Crete, Hiraklion, has one of the most extensive sewage systems in the world. www.knossos.com

4 Obviously, the technology for cleanliness was lost after the fall of the Roman Empire. As late as the 18th century in England, chamber pots (in-bedroom shit boxes and other liquids containers) were routinely tossed out of windows onto streets upon unsuspecting pedestrians. The phrase "The shit is flying! (sic)" can be traced to the Magna Carta (1512CE).

Thus, they wanted a shit house to take a proper, civilized shit. They also wanted a woman built like a brick shit house … and since they wanted both with near equal intensity, the two concepts were merged.[5]

Shit a brick

As a kid I thought this was the most painful thing I could imagine. I knew what a brick weighed, was also reasonably familiar with its dimensions and wondered how I could possibly survive such a maneuver. But I was reminded that women gave birth to babies with impossibly large heads, and I left it at that. Shitting a brick was a definite possibility.

It wasn't until a decade later that I learned that shitting a brick was a mental, not a physical, reaction to tension, worry, panic or eminent death.

DAMN, THAT WAS ROUGH!

"I shit a brick when I saw the shark clamp his jaws on my leg." Now this is an absolute perfect time to shit a brick.[6]

5 OK, OK. Before the femi-nazis come screaming, "built like a brick shit house" is a compliment. It does not disparage women (other than in the sexual object sense), and there is no implied scatological relationship.
6 Please, do not test this theory at home or while on the beach.

The shits

This is bad. Potentially fatal. Yes, Virginia, the shits can kill you.[7]

The shits begin like this: "Oh shit! I just *shat* my pants!" ("Just *shit* my pants" is also acceptable.) That's a case of the "Blitzkrieg Shits," for which you are totally unprepared, and you and your underwear both lose.

Or, the shits can begin with a low rumble, deep inside, just above your pelvic area. You wonder how no one else in the restaurant heard the cacophony. In automatic response, you look down and there it goes again, except there is a spontaneous contraction of the sphincter muscle. Then you consciously aid nature and intensify the contraction in the disappearing hope of forcing the intestinal tsunami back to whence it came. You throw your napkin down, try to slide your chair back delicately while calling in all powers of your gluteus maximus to provide additional tidal defense.

But your super-human efforts at forestalling the inevitable also further liquefied the onslaught, countering your best of intentions.

Knees together, bent over, hands indiscreetly placed, you make a run for the shitter. The restaurant patrons, including the mayor and Jerry Springer, can't help but notice that you squeak like a leaky balloon as you trot.[8]

"Oh Shit!" You don't know if you said it to yourself, in your head, or you are in the early stages of Tourette's. No matter.

The door … the WC door … you push (thankfully it is not a "pull") and Hallelujah! An empty stall … you unbelt and shift your body position by 180 degrees, tug down your drawers and then it's Vesuvius meets Niagara Falls.

Good thing you have a cell phone. "Hi, hon. Would you mind going to the car and bring me my jogging suit?"

---

7 Some deadly Diarrhea reference
8 The shits is also known as the trots because of the images such accidents conjure.

The "sharts"

A "Shart" is a combination of a shit and a fart. The two words are merely glued together. Of course, it could have been "fit" instead of "shart" but then the phrase "He's having a fit" would confuse the entire psychiatric community. So Shart it is.

Usually a shart occurs when one needs to fart, but knows there is a possibility of sewage leakage. The release of shit is unintentional (I hope) and the byproduct of nature telling us to sit down on a proper toilet for a few minutes.

I know that shart images are not pleasant at all, the same way skid marks on white underwear is pretty God awful, but we've all been there. Whether it is a case of the runs gone amok or an improperly sphinctorized wet one, the first thing you really want to do is take a shower … and maybe, just maybe, a proper shit.

The physics of sharts

Sharts can be easily categorized using the Standard Heterogeneous Interrelationship Tetrahedral approach to systems analysis. The four components are:

VELOCITY: There are two components here: The velocity of expelling air pressure through the lower intestine and the actual velocity of the ejecta material.

VOLUME: Shart volume varies greatly as the function $V = (f) [(T+P)-LF]$, where $T =$ the amount of time it takes to initiate and complete a sphincter grip, $P =$ the Pressure of the anal squeeze measured in **km/cm2** and $LF =$ Sphinctal Leak factor measured as **mm3/millisecond**.

VISCOSITY: The thickness or thinness of the shart material is a function of Pressure and Leak Factor divided by the initial projectile viscosity in the pre-sphincter chamber.

VENOM: In the Middle Ages, the French created a scheme to determine how much perfume was needed to cover up a given amount of body odor, and they called it "pewie." The deadliness of the shart odor is measured by the Pew-o-Meter, a highly sensitive piece of lab equipment that can measure pewies down to 3 sharts-per-billion!

A little SHART history:

The *Locus Classicus* of the new word *Shart* is a 2004 film script. I first heard it in this dialogue from the 2004 movie comedy *Along Came Polly* starring Ben Stiller, Jennifer Aniston and Philip Seymour Hoffman. Two old school buddies meet years after graduation. The character played by Hoffman is a vulgar professional buffoon, a slob and a failure who glommed one tiny moment of acting fame and then sank into deserved thespian obscurity.

Hoffman character: "We got to go, Dude!"

Ben Stiller character: "Why?"

Hoffman: "It's an emergency!"

Stiller: "What?"

Hoffman: (whispers) "I sharted, Dude."

Stiller: "What's *that*?"

Hoffman: "Sharted!"

Stiller: "Huh?"

Hoffman: "I farted and a little shit came out!"

Stiller: "You are the most disgusting person I've ever met in my life!"

The ultimate shart sound effects:

http://www.ebaumsworld.com/fartboard.html

The History of Shit.

As far as I can tell, shit began when a simple, post-amoebic, multicelled organism expelled a single cell as waste. That was shit. Of course, the quantum flux flotsam that ejects from a black hole could be called shit, but the math is way beyond me.

As life-forms evolved into more complex creatures, they consumed energy (food) and shat the useless bits out into the environment. Then some other low life-form would consume the first creature's shat shit (food), thus becoming the world's first shit eater (Dog owners will appreciate this).

Jurassic dinosaurs produced tons of shit daily. That was good for the plants. Dinosaur shit was plant food, much like cow shit grows tasty corn and dozens of other vegetables that adorn our dining table. Das right! The delicacies and food you eat are shit eaters in their own right, and you are … well … you can connect the dots without my help. (Shit eating humans, and that doesn't include professional scatologists.)

Rome, Crete – Sewage. They knew that shit flowed downhill, and Voila! Gravity was invented.

Middle Ages – out the windows. As the Roman Empire collapsed, control over (Western) civilization was assumed by a group of guys in Turkey, and

LOOK LIKE HIM NEED MORE FIBER!

they decided that the shit would hit the fan unless they invented the Catholic Church and the Holy Roman Empire. Charlemagne and all that. But somehow, the shit hitting the fan also meant the end of pagan Roman toilets and instead, the invention of chamber pots. One could quietly and privately shit to his heart's content into an awkward and very old ceramic pot, and then, after the deed was over, toss the shit out the window to Fleet Street, four floors below.

Where do you think fedoras (the hats) came from? Fedora is a French term meaning "Iron of Gold," which was the derogatory term for an alchemist's shit pile when failing to transmute iron or lead into gold. (Fe = abbreviation for ferrous (L) and d' = of and ora = gold.) So, the Fedora came to mean "shit protector." I guess words *do* change meaning over the centuries.

Indoor plumbing, it seems, was a forgotten science since the fall of Rome until the 19th Century in urban areas, and has still not found itself entrenched in townships like Green Acres, Hooterville and Mount Pilot. What can I say? The truth is, Opie shat in the woods or by the lake during commercial breaks.

THAT'S AL CAPONE AND HIS FAMOUS 'SHIT PROTECTOR' HAT. HECK, WITH AN "IRON OF GOLD" LIKE THAT, WHO NEEDS A BODY GUARD.

Thomas Crapper, 1836-1910; Sanitary Pioneer. Manufacturer, supplier and installer of sanitary goods (bathroom fittings, WCs etc.) plumbing and drainage. In other words, he is generally credited with inventing the modern shitter.[1]

1 http://www.thomas-crapper.com/history04.htm

S.H.I.T. is not an Acronym: The Etymology of Shit.

Fabulous bit of historical knowledge

Ever wonder where the word Shit comes from? Well, here it is:

Certain types of manure used to be transported (as everything was back then) by ship. In dry form it weighs a lot less, but once water (at sea) hit it, it not only became heavier, but the process of fermentation began again, of which a byproduct is methane gas.

As the stuff was stored below decks in bundles, you can see what could (and did) happen; methane gas began to build up below decks and the first time someone came below at night with a lantern … **BOOOOOM!**

Several ships were destroyed in this manner before it was discovered what was actually happening.

After that, the bundles of manure were always stamped with the term **S.H.I.T.** on them, which meant to the sailors to **"Ship High In Transit."** In other words, stored high enough off the lower decks so that any water that might come into the hold would not touch this volatile cargo and start the production of methane.

Bet you didn't know that one.

Here I always thought it was a golf term.

Another Origin Of shit

In the 1800s, cow pies were collected on the prairie and boxed and loaded onto steamships to burn instead of wood. Wood was not only hard to find, but heavy to move around and store.

When the boxes of cow pies were in the sun for days on end aboard the ships, they would smell bad. So when the manure was boxed up, they also stamped the outside of the box "S.H.I.T" or "Ship High In Transit." Now, when people came on board and said "Oh geeeez, what's that horrible smell," they were simply told it was shit.

That's where the saying *It smells like shit* came from.

Comments: Well, clever as that all is, etymologists everywhere must be holding their noses right about now. According to *my* dictionary, the word shit is much older than the 1800s, appearing in its earliest form – before 1,000 AD – as the Old English verb *scitan*. That's confirmed by lexicographer Hugh Rawson in his bawdily informative book *Wicked Words* (New York: Crown, 1989), where it is further noted that the expletive is a distant relative of words like *science, schedule* and *shield*. They all derive from the Indo-European root *skei-*, meaning to cut or to split. For most of its history "shit" was spelled shite (and sometimes still is euphemistically), but the modern spelling of the word can be found in texts dating as far back as the mid-1700s. It most certainly did not originate as an acronym.

Apropos that false premise, Rawson observed that shit has long been the subject of naughty wordplay, quite often based on made-up acronyms. For example:

In the Army, officers who did not go to West Point have been known to disparage the military academy as the South Hudson Institute of Technology. And, if an angelic 6-year-old asks, "Would you like to have some Sugar Honey and Iced Tea?" the safest course is to pretend that you have suddenly gone stone deaf.

And, finally, the "S.H.I.T." tale is reminiscent of another popular specimen of folk etymology claiming that the F-word (another good old-fashioned, all-purpose, four-letter expletive) originated as an acronym of "Fornication Under Consent of the King," or, in another variant, "For Unlawful Carnal Knowledge." Needless to say, it's all C.R.A.P.

http://urbanlegends.about.com/library/bl-s-word.htm

Greek: sk∂t∂

The most likely common word for shit in Proto-Indo-European would however probably be kakka (Cf. Latin Caca, Anglo-Saxon Cac, German Kacke, Kacken (*Pooh* or *to pooh*), or Cac (Dung), Greek Kakos (Bad).

BABIES KAKKA today. This clearly is another example that supports Carl Jung's hypothesis of the human archetype.

The word shit entered the modern English language, derived from the Old English nouns *scite* and the Middle Low German *schite*, both meaning "Dung," and the Old English noun *scitte*, meaning "diarrhea." Our most treasured cuss word has been with us a long, long time … showing up in written works both as a noun and as a verb as far back as the 14th century.

Scite can trace its roots back to the proto-Germanic root *skit-*, which brought us the German *scheisse*, Dutch *schijten*, Swedish *skita* and Danish *skide*. *Skit-* comes from the Indo-European root *skheid-* for "split, divide, separate," thus shit is distantly related to *schism* and *schist*. (If you're wondering what a verb root for the act of separating one thing from another would have to do with excrement, it was in the sense of the body's eliminating its waste — "separating" from it, so to speak.) Sort of the opposite of today's *getting one's shit together.*

Shit (v.)

O.E. *scitan*, from P. Gmc. *skit-*, from PIE *skheid-* "split, divide, separate." Related to *shed* (v.) on the notion of "separation" from the body (cf. L. *excrementum*, from *excernere* "to separate"). It is thus a cousin to *science* and *conscience*. The noun is O.E. *scitte* "purging"; sense of "excrement" dates from 1585, from the verb. <u>Despite what you read in an e-mail, "shit" is not an acronym</u>. The notion that it is a recent word may be because the word was taboo from c. 1600 and rarely appeared in print (neither Shakespeare nor the KJV has it), and even in "vulgar" publications of the late 18c. it is disguised by dashes. It drew the rath of censors as late as 1922 (*Ulysses* and *The Enormous Room*), scandalized magazine subscribers in 1957 (a Hemingway story *Atlantic Monthly*) and was omitted from some dictionaries as recently as 1970 (*Webster's New World*). Extensive slang usage; verb meaning "to lie, to tease" is from 1934; that of "to disrespect" is from 1903. Noun use for "obnoxious person" is since at least 1508; meaning "misfortune, trouble" is attested from 1937. *Shat* is a humorous past tense form, not etymological, first recorded 18c. *Shite*, now a jocular or slightly euphemistic variant, formerly a dialectal variant, reflects the vowel in the O.E. verb (cf. Ger. *scheissen*). *Shit-faced* drunk is 1960s student slang; shit list is from 1942. To *not give a shit* (not care) is from 1922; *up shit creek* (in trouble) is from 1937. *Scared shitless* was first recorded in 1936.

The expression *the shit hits the fan* is related to, and may well derive from, an old joke. A man in a crowded bar needed to defecate but couldn't find a bathroom, so he went upstairs and used a hole in the floor. Returning, he found everyone had gone except the bartender, who was cowering behind the bar. When the man asked what happened, the bartender replied, "Where were you when the shit hit the fan?" (Hugh Rawson, *Wicked Words*. 1989)

http://www.etymonline.com/index.php?term=shit

Random Shit and Shitty Acronyms

CRS: Can't Remember Shit. (**Note:** Remember the Michael Douglas movie *The Game?* The company that produced his "game" was named CRS, which was a clue to the movie's real meaning.

SAS (SASP): Sure As Shit (Positive)

SFB: Shit For Brains.
Any politician, boss or in-law.

SOL: Shit Outta Luck. If you don't know what this means already, then SAS, it's the same SOS; you really are SFB and SOL.

SOS: Same Old Shit.
What else can you expect?[1]

TS: Tough Shit

That_____is (for) Shit: That music is for shit. (*worse than sounds like shit.*) That steak is for shit. (Overcooked, too much gristle … whatever. It's for shit.)
   A perfect phrase to quickly demote just about anything to its scatological foundation.

---

1 Save Our Shit is an eco-friendly Green movement group operating out of Montana. They use the double entendre SOS to both vilify manure poaching and save the environment. A perfect example of a commercial enterprise using 'shit' as any term at all, in this case, the planet Earth.

That ain't (for) shit. That's useless. That's garbage. It's all lies. False advertising. Really shitty.

You ain't shit. You ain't nothing. You are sooooo low. I wouldn't even step on you. Feel bad? Good!

He ain't shit. (He ain't heavy. He's my brother.) Same shit as above.

SHIT IS NOT AN ACRONYM. SHIT IS NOT AN ACRONYM. SHIT IS NOT AN ACRONYM. SHIT IS NOT AN ACRONYM... SHIT... SHIT IS NOT AN ACRONYM. SHIT IS NOT AN ACRONYM. SHIT IS NOT AN ACRONYM... CRAP... SHIT IS NOT AN ACRONYM. SHIT IS NOT AN ACRONYM. SHIT IS NOT AN ACRONYM. SHIT IS NOT AN ACRONYM. DAMN IT TO HELL... SHIT IS NOT AN ACRONYM. SHIT IS NOT AN ACRONYM. SHIT IS NOT AN ACRONYM. SHIT IS NOT AN ACRONYM. SHIT IS NOT AN ACRO... HEY, I DON'T EVEN HAVE A COMPUTER AND ON TOP OF THAT, I DON'T EVEN KNOW WHAT A FREAKIN' ACRONYM IS... SHIT FIRE... LEMME OUTTA THIS MESS...

Fecalities[1]

THE GHOST SHIT: The kind where you feel shit come out, see shit on the toilet paper, but there's no shit in the bowl.

THE CLEAN SHIT: The kind where you feel shit come out, see shit in the bowl, but there's no shit on the toilet paper.

THE WET SHIT: You wipe your ass 50 times and it still feels unwiped. So you end up putting toilet paper between your ass and your underwear so you don't ruin them with skid marks.

THE SECOND WAVE SHIT: This shit happens when you've finished, your pants are up to your knees, and you suddenly realize you have to shit some more.

THE BRAIN HEMORRHAGE THROUGH YOUR NOSE SHIT: Also know as Pop a Vein in your Forehead Shit. You have to strain so much that you turn purple and have six cardiacs.

THE NOTORIOUS DRINKER SHIT: The kind of shit you have in the morning after a long night of drinking. It's most noticeable trait is the tread mark left on the bottom of the bowl after you flush.

THE "I REALLY WISH I COULD SHIT" SHIT: The kind where you want to shit, but even after straining your guts out, all you can do is sit on the toilet, cramped and farting out little pockets of air.

THE SWEET CORN SHIT: No explanation is necessary.

THE BIG LOG SHIT: The kind of shit that's so enormous, you're afraid to flush it down without first smashing it into little pieces with a toilet brush.

THE WET CHEEKS SHIT: Also known as the Power Dump. The kind that comes out of your ass so fast that

1 Stolen from somewhere on the Net. I don't know who to give credit to. Email me if you claim credit: **shittyauthor@theshitbook.com**

98

your butt cheeks get splashed with toilet water.

THE LIQUID SHIT: That's the kind where yellowish-brown liquid shoots out of your hole, splashes all over the side of the toilet bowl like a dropped bowl of Bolognaise and, at the same time, gives third-degree burns to your ringpiece.

THE MEXICAN FOOD SHIT:
This is in a class all its own.

THE CROWD PLEASER: This shit is so intriguing in size and/or appearance that you have to show it off to someone before flushing it away.

THE MOOD ENHANCER: This shit occurs after a lengthy period of constipation, thereby allowing you to be your old self again.

THE RITUAL: This shit occurs at the same time each day and it is accomplished with the aid of a newspaper.

THE GUINESS BOOK OF RECORDS SHIT: A shit so noteworthy it should be recorded for future generations.

THE AFTERSHOCK SHIT: This shit has an odor so powerful, that anyone entering the vicinity within the next 7 hours is affected.

THE "HONEYMOON'S OVER" SHIT:
This is any shit created in the presence of another person.

THE GROANER: A shit so huge that it cannot exit without vocal assistance.

THE FLOATER: Characterized by its floatability, this shit has been known to tumble and swirl and resurface after many flushings.

THE BOMBSHELL: A shit that comes as a complete surprise at a time that is either inappropriate to shit (i.e., during lovemaking or a root canal) or you are nowhere near shitting facilities.

THE OLYMPIC SHIT: This shit occurs exactly one hour prior to the start of any competitive event in which you are entered and bears a close resemblance to the Drinker's Shit.

THE BACK-TO-NATURE SHIT: This shit may be of any variety but is always deposited either in the woods or while hiding behind the passenger side of your car.

THE SNAKE CHARMER: A long and skinny shit which has managed to coil itself into a frightening position, but usually harmless.

THE PEBBLES-FROM-HEAVEN SHIT: An adorable collection of small turds in a cluster, often a gift from God when you actually CAN'T shit.

THE RANGER: A shit which refuses to let go. It is usually necessary to engage a rocking and bouncing motion, but quite often the only solution is to push it away with a piece of toilet paper.

THE PHANTOM SHIT: This appears in the toilet mysteriously and nobody admits to putting it there.

THE PEEK-A-BOO SHIT: Now you see it. Now you don't. This shit is playing games with you. Requires patience & muscle control.

PREMEDITATED SHIT: Laxative-induced. Doesn't count.

SHITZOPHRENIA: Fear of shitting. Can be fatal!

ENERGIZER SHIT: Also known as a "Still Going" shit.

THE POWER DUMP SHIT: The kind that comes out so fast, you barely get your pants down.

THE LIQUID PLUMMER SHIT: This kind of shit is so freaking big it plugs up the toilet and it eventually overflows all over the bathroom floor.

THE SPINAL TAP SHIT: The kind of shit that hurts so much coming out, you'd swear it has to be coming out sideways.

THE "I THINK I'M GIVING BIRTH THROUGH MY ASSHOLE" SHIT: Similar to the Spinal Tap Shit. The shape and size of the turd resembles a beer can. Vacuous air space remains in the rectum for some time afterwards.

THE PORRIDGE SHIT: The type that comes out like toothpaste, and just keeps coming. You have two choices: **(1)** Flush and keep going or **(2)** Risk it piling up to your bum while you sit there helpless.

THE "I'M GOING TO CHEW MY FOOD BETTER" SHIT: When the bag of Stackers you ate last night lacerates the insides of your rectum on the way out in the morning.

THE "I THINK I'M TURNING INTO A BUNNY" SHIT: When you drop lots of cute, little round ones that look like marbles and make tiny plopping sounds.

THE "WHAT THE HELL DIED IN HERE" SHIT: Also referred to as The Toxic Dump. Of course you don't warn anyone of the poisonous odor. Instead, you stand innocently near the door and enjoy the show as they run out gasping for air.

THE "I JUST KNOW THERE'S A TURD STILL DANGLING THERE" SHIT: Where you just sit there patiently and wait for the last cling-on to drop off because if you wipe now, it'll smear all over the place.

THE "DAIRY QUEEN DIP" SHIT: Similar to the Snake Charmer Shit, with the coiling action, but looks more like a soft ice cream from your local neighborhood ice cream parlor. Cones optional.

The Future of Shit

Some writers call this last section of a book "Summary" or "Epilogue" or "In Conclusion" or some shit like that. But I am The Shitty Author, and as such, thought I'd share The Future of Shit with you.

First, our website is **www.theshitbook.com** so come on down and look at our shit.

Second, I can't personally know about all the shit in the world (I admit it, Honey!), so I want all of you to think about shit and send it to me. This will help with future books. I won't pay you since I do most of the work, not including the work of the Shitty Artist, but I'll include your name, e-mail and if you submit a real shitty picture that meets our ethical and disgust-level criteria, we might use that too.

Here are the upcoming books:

Shit and More Shit

Send me those shitty applications in English, please! When I receive enough new uses of or for shit, I'll publish them and make another $1.381 or such.

1. Shitty euphemisms
2. Add to our taxonomy or create a new category!

Foreign Shit

Merde, France! Give us your shit! By God, your country does it anyway!

Skata, Greece! Ever notice that scatology, et al, are based upon your ancient ways; and Hey! What's with those naked male Olympic athletes? Doesn't that flip-flop slow them down on the track?

You get the idea! By country, language or topic … I don't give a shit.

Squatter's writes: Shitters in history

My mother began this project before she passed. Time to finish it with your help.

1. Historical scatology

2. Really weird shit in bathroom, strange plumbing. (Sort of like the gravity flow, sand urinals in Egypt. I didn't take a shit though. Too feline.)

> ∿My Diary – King Tut
>
> Gravity is the sure solution for workers waste while high on the pyramids. Long slides can be built so that when
>
> Excuse me. I have to take a shit.

Thanks a Shitload!

From the Shitty Author
and the Really Shitty Artist.

FUTURE SHIT: Your Shitty Ideas!